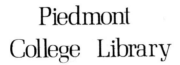

Child Management
A Program for Parents and Teachers

Judith M. Smith and Donald E. P. Smith

Research Press Company
2612 North Mattis Avenue, Champaign, Illinois 61820

3/8/78 ord. 3.9ʃ

ISBN 0-87822-125-5

Library of Congress Catalog Card Number 76-22829

Contents

PREFACE

This self-instruction booklet is designed for parents and other child care specialists. Its immediate objective is to provide a technique for handling certain problems of child management. Its ultimate objective is to provide parents with a systematic point of view for interpreting behavior so that they can create a healthy learning environment.

The principles illustrated herein derive from recent research in behavioral science, particularly from that branch called behavior technology. Since the original edition appeared in 1966, these principles have been put into practice successfully by tens of thousands of parents both in this country and abroad.

The Reader Is Strongly Advised to Proceed as Follows:

1. Start at the beginning and read consecutively. (Later sections depend on mastery of the first sections.)
2. Do not institute changes in your management practices until you complete the book.
3. Read only a few pages at one sitting. For example:
   1st day—Chapter 1 (entire)
   2nd day—Chapter 2, pages 19-32
   3rd day—Chapter 2, pages 33-73
   4th day—Chapter 3, pages 75-92
   5th day—Chapter 3, pages 93-112
   Black edging on a page indicates a new day's work.
4. Record your answers on a separate sheet, or in the book.

For professional advice, contact your school or physician who will provide the name of a psychologist or psychiatrist.

VALIDATION

Child Management is a course of instruction designed to improve the skill of parents and teachers in training children. Its effectiveness has been determined in three ways: (1) the accuracy of responses within the material; (2) the improvement in scores on a test of child rearing practices taken before and after reading the material; and (3) report of changes in behavior by parents and teachers two weeks after reading the material.

ACCURACY OF RESPONSES

In a trial with 30 parents of average and above average socio-economic level, 96.4% of the responses within the program were correct. Problem items were revised.

An answer key is provided in the current edition.

IMPROVEMENT IN SCORES ON A TEST OF CHILD REARING PRACTICES

A 10-question objective test was given to 36 teachers and parents. Average scores were as follows:

Pretest–37.5% (S. D. 4.5)
Posttest–85.5% (S. D. 6.2)

The scores were distributed as follows:

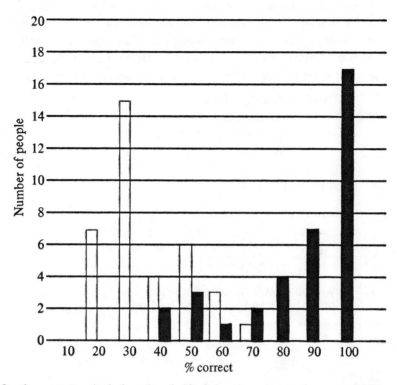

On the pretest, a little less than half of the group received scores of 30%. On the posttest, about half scored 100%.

CHANGES IN BEHAVIOR

A questionnaire was given to 50 members of a graduate course called "Basic Conepts in School Learning." Of the total, 15 were teaching in public schools, 2 in a school for emotionally disturbed children, one was a teacher of adults, and one was a social case worker. Thirteen were parents, several were married but without children and 17 were single persons who were full-time students. Of the single students, 14 reported no opportunity to use the techniques described in the material.

The following results are, for the most part, based upon 36 parents and teachers who had an opportunity to use the techniques.

1. "Have You Experienced Insights?"

	Yes	No
Kinds of insights:	33	3

"I do too much nagging" (2); "Understand reason for my child's cursing"; "Large number of rules people use which are ineffectual" (2); "Power of the parent is frightening"; "My child's pleasure when he knows the limits"; "Obvious now that my children's misbehavior was rule-testing and we kept changing the rules"; "My nagging was unnecessary when I enforced the rule"; "Situations control children"; "My spontaneous behavior was usually the wrong one"; "I've been reinforcing unwanted behaviors"; etc.

2. "Did You Establish A Rule?"

			Yes	No
"For whom?"	School class:	10	26	9
	Own children:	12		
	Spouse:	2		
	Roommate:	1		
	Pet:	1		

3. "Future Plans (Concerning the Rule)?"

In all cases, subjects reported that they intended to continue the new practice. Of the 9 who reported that they had not established a rule, 4 stated that they already followed the procedure.

4. "How Would You Assess Changes in Your Ability to Cope with Children?"

(All 50 subjects responded.)

	Less able	Possibly less able	No change	Possibly more able	More able
Number responding:	0	0	11	22	17

5. "Impressions Which May Be Relevant?"

The following two comments reflect recurrent themes reported by the subjects:

"The relationship between my son and me has improved as it has between son and father, creating a more comfortable family situation ... has enabled us to allow him more independence, more freedom to grow through experience, a most worthwhile change." "I feel more in control of the group of emotionally disturbed children I teach. I'm more even-tempered (feel calmer) and more objective. One child's temper tantrums have been decreasing in time and frequency, from 45 minutes to 1 or 2 minutes. His behavior is improving. In general, much testing behavior is decreasing, such as running away from adults, crawling under tables, into closets, etc. I'm impressed with progress so far."

1

CONSISTENCY IN PARENT BEHAVIOR

WHY DO CHILDREN ACT THAT WAY?

To begin with, children are neither good nor bad. If they are usually happy, lively, and a joy to be with, their parents have helped to make them that way. If they are usually irritable, fearful, obstinate, or sly, their parents have helped to make them that way. Not knowingly, of course. Parents arrange situations in which learning takes place. Often the arrangement is accidental and learning occurs which we don't want.

For example, a child will repeat a behavior which makes him feel good. When he expects his behavior to have a certain consequence, and it does, he feels good—and tends to repeat the behavior.

1. When he comes home from school, he calls out "Mom?" He expects her to answer. She calls "I'm out here!" He smiles. He feels good. He expected her to answer—and she did answer. He will be more likely to call out "Mom?" when he comes home tomorrow.

2. When he comes home later than usual, he expects her to notice it. She says "You're late." He feels good. He expected a consequence, and it occurred. He will be more likely to come home late tomorrow.

When an expected consequence of a behavior does not occur, the behavior tends not to be repeated.

1. When he comes home from school and calls out "Mom?" he receives no answer. He expected her to answer and she did not. She wasn't there. He becomes upset and the tendency to call out "Mom?" on arrival from school is weakened.

2. When he comes home later than usual, he expects his mother to notice. If she does not comment on his lateness, the expected consequence does not occur. He "looks angry," pouts, or expresses disappointment. "Coming home later than usual" tends to be weakened.

In each situation, which response will make the behavior *less* likely in the future? (Circle *a* or *b* and record your answer on the answer sheet.)

---

1 | Sam "kids" the office secretary by making slightly off-color remarks.
  a. She blushes and says "You shouldn't talk like that."
  ✗ b. She appears to be engrossed in her work.

Record your answer.

---

2 | Darlene (age 3) pushes the doorbell repeatedly.
  ✗ a. Mother does not go to the door.
  b. Mother opens the door.

Record your answer.

---

3 | Mark called his sister a dummy.
  ✗ a. Sister didn't seem to hear.
  b. Sister began to cry and ran to Mother to complain.

Record your answer.

A behavior is strengthened when we expect some result to happen—and it does. A behavior is weakened when we expect some result to happen—and it doesn't. This law of behavior provides a powerful tool for child training. Commonly, what the child expects is some response by his parent. Thus the parent can strengthen or weaken certain behaviors by controlling her own response to that behavior. She can do much more. By behaving consistently in certain situations, she can stabilize an important part of her child's emotional life.

What Is Consistency?

Consistency means the *absolute* predictability of a parent's behavior. To the child it means "*Every* time I fail to do the dishes before I go to bed, Mother will get me out of bed to do them." Or, "*Every* time I am late for dinner, I will get nothing to eat." Or, "*Every* time I get out of bed at night, Dad will put me in again."

To the parent it means "*Every* time Johnny asks for candy before supper, I will say 'No'." Or, "*Every* time Mary attacks her baby brother, I will remove one of them." Or, "I will *always* insist that Jill clean her room on Tuesday evening before she joins the family for dinner."

In which situation below does the parent act consistently? (Circle *a* or *b*.)

4

a. Monday—nap time. 2:15 P.M. Jack gets out of his bed. Mother calls "Get back in bed, Jack." Ten minutes later he is still up. She puts him back in bed. He goes to sleep.

Tuesday—nap time. 2:10 P.M. Jack gets out of bed. Mother puts him back immediately.
2:30 P.M. He gets out again. Mother is busy ironing and Jack is playing quietly. She does nothing. At 2:51 he starts pounding the wall. She quickly puts him back to bed. He goes to sleep.

Wednesday—nap time. 2:12 P.M. Jack gets out of bed and begins pounding the wall. Mother calls "Jack, you stop that noise and get into bed."
2:15 P.M. The pounding begins again. Mother calls "Jack, I told you to get in that bed and stay there."
2:20 P.M. Jack begins opening and closing the closet door. Mother puts him back to bed. He goes to sleep.

b. Monday—nap time. 2:15 P.M. Joey gets out of bed. Father puts him back immediately, saying "It's not time to get up yet." He goes to sleep.

Tuesday—nap time. 2:10 P.M. Joey gets out of bed. Father puts him back, saying "It's not time to get up yet."
2:30 P.M. Joey gets out again. Father puts him back, saying "It's not time to get up yet." He goes to sleep.

Wednesday—nap time. 2:12 P.M. Joey calls out "Is it time to get up?" Father answers "No." He goes to sleep.

Record your answer.

In which of the situations below do the parents behave consistently?

5   a. Monday—Dinner is ready but Linda is not home. Linda knows that dinner is always served at 6:30, and she can tell time. The family sits down to eat without her. She arrives at 6:33.

Tuesday—Linda is on time for dinner.

Wednesday—Linda arrives at 6:55. The food is all gone. She fixes herself some corn flakes.

Thursday—Linda is 10 minutes late for dinner. Her milk is warm and the potatoes are gone.

Friday—Linda is on time for dinner.

- -

   b. Monday—Dinner is ready but Laura is not home. Dinner is always served at 6:30, and Laura can tell time. Mother calls her in from outside. She appears in 3 minutes and the family begins eating.

Tuesday—Laura is in the house at dinner time.

Wednesday—Laura is late for dinner. At 6:32 Mother calls outside. There is no response. At 6:41 Father calls. Mother puts her food in the oven. At 6:53 Father searches the neighborhood and brings her home.

Thursday—Laura is not home at 6:30. Mother phones the friend she is visiting. Laura promises to come right home. She still has not arrived at 6:40, so the family sits down to eat. There is nothing left when she arrives at 6:57. After a tantrum, she fixes herself a bowl of corn flakes.

Friday—Laura is not home at 6:30. Mother sends Father out to find her. He brings her back at 6:34.

Why Is Consistency Important?

People have certain obvious needs—food, shelter, sex. But they have another need that is not discussed very often—a need for safety. The world around us is full of danger, and the body remains constantly ready to react to a threat. The heart speeds up, pupils dilate, blood moves away from the hands and feet. This is an uncomfortable condition. In extreme instances, it contributes to asthma, nightmares, hives, and temper tantrums. We can relieve the discomfort of being "constantly ready" to defend ourselves by predicting what will happen next. If our predictions come true, we feel safe. If they don't come true, it is upsetting—we become angry. If we can't make any successful predictions at all, we are in a constant state of turmoil.

To a child, the adults having authority over her are the main sources of threat, just as they are the main sources of comfort and nurturance. If much of their behavior is consistent and predictable, she feels safe. She need not spend all her energy figuring out what Mom is going to do next. She can concentrate on determining what other events in her world are predictable. That is, she is free to explore the world and to learn about it.

If her parents are unpredictable, she feels chronically anxious. Every time Dad states a rule ("Be home by 5:00," "Don't hit your brother," etc.), she must test that rule. And every time Dad does not enforce the rule, the child's anxiety rises. She may, in time, become a master at manipulating her parents—usually by doing all the things that upset them. Getting angry is the most consistent thing most parents do. She must produce that consistency. However, she usually has little energy left for dealing with the rest of her environment.

You may be thinking "But life is not completely predictable and people are not always dependable. One must learn to cope." That is true, of course. And it is because life is so unpredictable that a few points of consistency are so important. It would be impossible (and undesirable) to behave consistently in all situations. Still, if a parent can become consistent in just one or two behaviors, he becomes a reliable person in a child's eyes. Then the child can afford to abandon many of her testing behaviors, and can cope more effectively in all areas.

Which of the behaviors below provides the greater consistency in the environment? (Circle *a* or *b*.)

6
  a. Serving dinner at exactly 6:00 every night.
  b. Serving dinner when everybody is ready.

7
  a. Giving Warren 50 cents a week as an allowance.
  b. Giving Warren money when he needs it.

8
  a. Giving Julie a bath every night.
  b. Giving Julie a bath when she is dirty.

9
  a. Insisting that Martha clean her room whenever it becomes intolerably dirty.
  b. Insisting that Martha clean her room every Saturday, whether it seems to need it or not.

WHAT IS THE RESULT OF CONSISTENCY?

Whenever a change occurs in the child's environment, his whole world becomes unpredictable. An emotional response to this unpredictability will occur. With children it takes the form of temper tantrums or, sometimes, of illness. Older children and adults experience feelings of anger, frustration and fear, or sometimes illness.

When a child's life has no important points of consistency, his predictions are constantly unfulfilled. He experiences tantrums or illness often. Suppose a parent introduces some important new consistency into the environment. This is a crucial change in a child's life, and it will be met with the inevitable tantrums. As soon as the "new way" becomes predictable, however, the tantrums will decrease.

The temper tantrum, then, is a symptom of an unfulfilled expectancy—a prediction that does not come true. When Mother behaves differently, when the furniture is rearranged, even when the weather changes, a child (or an adult) feels upset. A tantrum is likely to occur. Many tantrums could be avoided by adhering to established routines. And when routines must be changed, parents can anticipate a child's reaction and take it in stride.

Temper tantrums are probably more than just a symptom of a child's unfulfilled expectations. They serve to weaken an unrealistic prediction (it is unrealistic since the expected result did not happen). Thus, the next time the event occurs, a tantrum is less likely. Knowing that they are inevitable, necessary, and predictable makes temper tantrums easier to tolerate.

A number of situations are described below. After each description you will find two interpretations of the situation. Choose the interpretation which is based on the foregoing discussion of consistency and predictability. (Note: the other choice is not necessarily untrue or unreasonable.) Circle *a* or *b*.

10 | Mother fastens a brand new bib around baby's neck. She starts to feed him his favorite—chicken and vegetables. Baby cries and refuses to eat anything.
　　a. Baby expected his old, familiar bib.
　　b. Baby doesn't like chicken and vegetables.

11 | Father always serves breakfast at 8:05—just after Captain Kangaroo comes on. This morning he is in a hurry and breakfast is ready at 7:30. Two-year-old Marilyn fidgets, eats very little, cries loudly when she drops her spoon.
　　a. Marilyn is coming down with a cold.
　　b. The early breakfast upset Marilyn's expectations.

12 | Mark insists that his parents read the same story, night after night.
　　a. Mark is not very bright.
　　b. It is comforting and relaxing to know what is coming next in the story.

13 | The substitute teacher sent George (age 6) home at 10:00 A.M. He had complained of a severe stomachache. At home he seems perfectly well.
　　a. George took advantage of the teacher to get a day off.
　　b. George's stomachache was a result of an upsetting change in his environment—the substitute teacher.

14 | Mother: "Why is it that every time I feel bad the kids are at their worst? This morning I felt sick. Tom and Ann fought all. morning. Blake found a crayon and wrote all over the wall. Dee was 10 minutes late for school."
- a. The children are all reacting to a change in the way Mother looks and acts.
- b. The children wait until Mother is feeling bad to try getting away with their bad behavior.

15 | In spite of all the gifts Jack got for Christmas, he became very angry when he did not get a particular model car he wanted.
- a. His tantrum was a result of a strong expectation that was not fulfilled.
- b. He is a selfish and ungrateful child.

16 | Geraldine has been moping around the house for days because Brian didn't ask her to the prom. The funny thing is, she refused a date with him last weekend to go out with another boy.
- a. She wants only what she can't have.
- b. She had expected Brian to ask her, and his failure to call is upsetting.

17 | Barbara burst into tears when she received a B+ on her exam.
- a. She was quite certain she had gotten an A.
- b. She was making a play for sympathy in hopes that her teacher would change her grade.

18 | Mother became quite angry when 12-year-old Candice appeared for breakfast wearing lipstick.
- a. Mother was upset because Candice looked greatly different from the way she usually looked in the morning.
- b. Mother is afraid to let Candice grow up.

How Does a Child React to a New Environment?

TESTING OLD RULES

An environment is "new" whenever a part of it changes. It is a new environment when the family moves to a new house, when Mother brings home a baby brother, when Dad is worried, when the first winter snowstorm occurs. A child must immediately determine the points of predictability in the new environment. This usually means that she systematically breaks all the established rules—to find out if they are still in force. Then she experiments—to find out if there are any new ones. For reasons discussed previously, tantrums are likely if there are changes.

We may conclude, then, that it is especially important for parents to provide consistency whenever there is a change in the environment. Unfortunately, this is usually the time when parents are inconsistent. They do not enforce the usual rules, perhaps because they are sick and don't have the energy, or because Johnny has so many other demands on him, or because he is acting so strangely that *he* must be sick.

As well as testing all the rules, a child will attempt to change things back to the previous condition. He may not have been happy with the old way, but at least it was familiar. Therefore, Johnny steadfastly ignores the new baby, or he attacks it, or asks Mom to take it back. Willy may insist that his new room be arranged just like the old one. When Dad lies on the couch to relieve his aching back, Bonnie climbs on him and pesters him until he sits up. Then she pleads "Smile, Daddy. Don't be mad." Eddie, whose mother has abandoned spanking as a form of punishment, commits every crime in his repertoire, and finally says "Mom, I really think I need a spanking today." A mother insists that her rapidly maturing teen-age daughter wear juvenile clothes.

In all of these examples, the upsetting thing is not that the new situation is undesirable. The problem arises from the fact that the new situation is a change from the old.

Several situations are described below. Choose the interpretation that is consistent with the preceding discussion.

19 | There is a substitute teacher in the third grade class today. The children talk out of turn, throw paper wads, and do poorly on their work.
   a. The children dislike the substitute.
   b. The children are discovering which rules are still in force in the classroom.

20 | Mr. Brown's children are usually well behaved. But when he left them with a new baby-sitter, they acted very badly—refused to go to bed on time, didn't pick up their toys, and fought with each other.
   a. The children were finding out which rules the baby-sitter would establish.
   b. The baby-sitter must be incompetent if such behavior occurred.

21 | When Jimmy's parents took him out to dinner, he picked at his food restlessly, dropped his silverware, fidgeted in his chair. Finally, he poured his milk into his plate. The parents, not wishing to cause a scene, said nothing. Then he demanded another glass of milk. When he started to pour this one into his plate, too, Dad stopped him. Jimmy threw a temper tantrum.
   a. Jimmy's parents have failed to teach him good table manners.
   b. Jimmy was upset by eating in a strange place. He was further upset by Dad's inconsistent response to pouring milk into a plate.

TESTING A NEW RULE

Suppose a parent states a new rule, such as "You must clean your room every Saturday before you go out to play." Or "If you spill your milk again, you will have to clean it up." This new rule creates a new environment, which must be tested. A child must break the rule—usually several times—before he is sure it is truly in effect. If parents enforce the rule consistently, the child will stop testing it. From time to time, when he is feeling anxious, he will test it again, just as he tests other rules when the environment changes. If the parents do not enforce the new rule consistently, the child is never free to stop testing it.

Two situations are described on the next page. Circle the one in which the parents acted consistently.

a. Tom was given the job of emptying the trash. He had to finish the chore before he could watch his favorite TV program at 7:00 in the evening.

Monday: Tom emptied the trash at 6:30.

Tuesday: At 6:58, Tom asked if he could wait until after the program tonight because he forgot about the trash. Parents said "No." Tom stomped out angrily, slamming the door. He finished at 7:08.

Wednesday: Tom was not feeling well. He was very tired, had a temperature, and other cold symptoms. Parents did not require him to empty the trash.

Thursday: Tom delayed emptying the trash until 7:00. Complained of feeling dizzy. Parents said "No trash, no TV." Muttering angrily against unfair parents, Tom emptied the trash.

Friday: Tom started to watch a special educational program at 6:30. Parents did not want to interrupt him until the end of the program so they waited until 7:30 before reminding him about the trash.

----

b. Steve had to empty the trash before 7:00, or no TV.

Monday: Steve emptied the trash at 6:45.

Tuesday: Steve forgot until 6:58. Parents said nothing, but turned off the TV at 7:00. Steve stomped and cursed under his breath. He finished at 7:12.

Wednesday: Steve had a temperature and other cold symptoms. Parents turned off TV at 7:00. Steve emptied the trash, muttering against cruel parents who want their children to get pneumonia.

Thursday: Steve emptied trash at 6:49.

Friday: At 7:00, Steve turned off TV and emptied trash.

2

USING RULES
TO PROVIDE CONSISTENCY

In the first section of this program you learned that consistency in parental behavior makes the world safer for children. Parents can become more consistent by establishing a few rules and enforcing them absolutely. Most parents have far too many rules, and they don't enforce any of them consistently. In that case, rules make life more complicated for everybody. In this section, you will learn what kind of rules should be established and how they should be enforced.

WHAT IS A RULE?

Any demand made on a child by a parent is a rule. Any task he must perform is a rule. Any decision regarding what he may have or may not have, what he may do or may not do—any such decision is a rule. Many parents dislike establishing rules. Usually they feel guilty when they require the child to do something which is unpleasant. They are not aware that consistent enforcement of a rule makes the world safer and more comfortable for the child.

Parents sometimes disguise rules to ease their guilt. They say "Wouldn't you like to do the dishes?" Or "Do you want to take a nap?" If the only acceptable answer to the question is "yes," it is a rule—regardless of the way it is stated. It would be much less confusing to the child if Mother said "Do the dishes now." Or "It's naptime."

Some rules are "long term." They must be enforced again and again over a long period of time. These rules usually govern the performance of a chore or a family routine. In each item below, choose the long-term rule.

23 | a. Mark must cut the grass every Saturday afternoon.
b. Mark can earn 50 cents by weeding the garden.

24 | a. Mother provides Joan with an alarm clock.
b. Joan must dress herself without help before she leaves for school.

25 | a. John has to do the dishes on Monday and Friday.
b. John's brother asks him to substitute for him on Wednesday.

26 | a. Everyone must wash his hands and face before eating dinner.
b. It is often necessary to turn on the light in the dining room if the sun has set.

Short-term rules, or *commands,* are less easily recognized as rules. These are the spontaneous decisions of parents peculiar to particular situations. They require consistent enforcement just as do long-term rules. They are often harder to enforce because they have not been carefully planned. Often they are impossible to enforce. In each item below, circle the *command.*

27
a. "You may not have a cookie before dinner."
b. "We are having roast chicken for dinner."

28
a. "That dress looks nice on you."
b. "Wash your face."

29
a. "Look at it rain!"
b. "Don't climb over the fence."

30
a. "Give Jackie his fire engine."
b. "Do you like that fire engine?"

31 | a. "Why don't you let George have a turn?"
b. "Isn't it a nice day today?"

32 | a. "What would you like for lunch today?"
b. "Don't you think it would be nice to have lunch now?"

33 | a. "Be home by 12:30."
b. "Lunch will be served at 12:30."

34 | a. "Your shirt is dirty."
b. "Change that shirt before you leave."

35 | a. "I hope you don't fall off the swing."
b. "Don't swing so high."

36 | a. "Say 'Thank you' to the lady."
b. "Would you like one of the lady's balloons?"

37 | a. "Come in the house now."
b. " 'Lassie' is on TV now."

WHAT KIND OF RULES?

A parent may decide to increase the consistency in a child's life. One effective way to start is by establishing a long-term rule, usually a household chore, and by enforcing it consistently. The rule must be chosen very carefully. A good rule must fulfill three requirements. It must be definable. It must be reasonable. It must be enforceable.

Choosing a Definable Rule

Mrs. Johnson tells her daughter "From now on, you must look decent before you leave the house." That rule sounds reasonable until you try to define just what Mrs. Johnson means by "look decent." Perhaps she means that her clothes must be clean and pressed. But what about the crease in her skirt from sitting down, or the small orange juice spot from breakfast? Is yesterday's blouse clean enough? How often must you wear a skirt before it's dirty? And what about her shoes, hair, make-up? Can she wear that awful sweater she bought last week, even if it *is* clean? And what about that skirt that is really too tight?

Only Mrs. Johnson knows what she means by "look decent." And the chances are that her evaluation of an outfit varies from day to day. Her daughter certainly can't predict whether she will pass inspection. So this rule is worse than no rule at all. It creates uncertainty rather than reducing it.

If a rule is well defined, the child knows instantly when he has broken it (and he will have to break it to test it). He may argue that you are unreasonable, but he cannot argue that he has already fulfilled the requirements. For example, Mother tells Pete "From now on, you must empty the trash before bedtime. That includes the baskets in the kitchen, bathroom and family room. It also includes lighting the incinerator." Pete knows exactly what he has to do—empty three baskets and light the incinerator. He also knows when he has to do it—every night before bedtime. If he does not fulfill any part of the routine, his parents will enforce the rule.

Monday: Pete empties the baskets and lights the incinerator. His parents say nothing.

Tuesday: Pete does not light the incinerator. Mother discovers this at 9:30, when Pete is in pajamas. She says "Pete, you haven't finished your chore." Pete replies, incredulously, "You mean I have to go out there now? I'm not even dressed." Mother: "You must finish your chore."

Wednesday: Pete does not empty the bathroom basket since there are only a few pieces of paper in it. Dad discovers it and says "Pete, you haven't finished your chore." Pete complies.

Parents must be willing to live with their definition of the chore. They can demand no more than (and no less than) exact fulfillment of the stated requirements. Pete, for example, performed his chore without incident for several weeks. Then one night he left all three baskets in the kitchen. Mother said nothing since she had not told him that returning the baskets was a part of the job. Pete repeated this behavior the next night. Mom said nothing. The third night he left them out by the incinerator. Mom said nothing, but decided to change the rule. The next day she said to him "Pete, from now on you must return the baskets to their proper places." Pete complied.

Several rules are stated below. In each item, circle the one which is definable.

38
a. "Tim, the dishes must be done before you go to bed. By that I mean everything has to be in place and the kitchen must look neat."
b. "Tim, the dishes must be done before you go to bed. I will post this check list of what must be done."

Check List

Dishes, silverware, and pans washed, dried, and put away.
Counter washed.
Sink scoured.
Garbage wrapped.
Tea kettle filled.
Soap, dish pan, towels, and dish rags put away.

39
a. "Betty, I want you to cut the grass every Friday afternoon. Do the back yard, front yard, and front extension. Also, edge the front sidewalk on both sides, and clip around the trees."
b. "Betty, I want you to cut the grass every Friday afternoon. And I want you to do a thorough job. None of this slapdash stuff."

40
a. "Kathy, your job will be dusting the living room on Monday and Friday. Dust all the wood, the baseboard, and the leather chair. On Friday, use furniture polish."
b. "Kathy, your job will be dusting the living room on Monday and Friday. You can use furniture polish on Friday. And remember, anything worth doing is worth doing well."

Choosing a Reasonable Rule

When parents establish a rule of the type we are discussing, they do it to make the environment more comfortable for the child. When the child follows the rule, he is performing a normal, necessary function. He is not being a good boy or helping mother.

How much time? When the rule concerns a chore, the length of time it takes is probably of little importance. To increase stability, making the bed every day may be as effective as doing the dishes every day. First, determine how much time it will take. Then, determine how much time is available, allowing plenty for playing, resting, and studying.

Can he do it? Is he capable of performing the chore? Making a bed may seem like a simple job, but watching a child attempt it for the first time will convince you otherwise. You may very well have to teach the child how to perform the task, even if it is a simple one. Children often don't know where to begin. One way of teaching a task is described below. Following this procedure will avoid arguments, tears, and resentment. First, list all the steps in performing the task (this list is for you, not the child). On the first day have the child sit and watch while you perform all but the very last step. Be sure the last step is very simple. Tell him what to do, and leave the room.

On the second day, the child watches while you do all but the last 2 steps. You leave the room while he finishes.

On the third day the child performs the last 3 steps after you leave.

Continue this procedure until he is doing the whole thing himself.

The child may call you back to inspect the finished product, but it is important that you *do not* watch him actually do the steps. It is also wise not to comment on the finished product unless he asks you. In that case, say "It's fine," and do not mention the minor flaws. He will correct them as he becomes more skillful. If he has failed to perform a whole step, simply say "You haven't finished," and leave so that he can complete his work.

An example of this method is described below.

Mother made out the following list to guide her in teaching Janie to make her bed:

1. Remove pillow and put it on the chair.
2. Pull bed out from the wall.
3. Throw back covers.
4. Smooth bottom sheet.
5. Bring top sheet up and smooth it.
6. Bring up blankets and smooth them.
7. Tuck in blankets that have pulled out at the foot of the bed.
8. Turn square corners at the foot of bed.
9. Turn back sheet over blankets (about 3 inches).
10. Bring up bedspread and turn it back 12 inches from head of the bed.
11. Smooth and straighten bedspread.
12. Replace pillow.
13. Bring bedspread up over pillow.
14. Push bed back to the wall.

On Sunday, Mother performed steps 1 through 13 while Janie watched. She left and Janie pushed the bed to the wall. On Monday, Mother did steps 1 through 12 and Janie did 13 and 14. This procedure continued, with Janie doing one more step each day. On the seventh day, Janie stopped Mother after she finished step 4, saying, "I can do the rest." Mother left the room. On the eighth day Janie wanted to do the whole thing by herself, which she did quite adequately.

Mother wanted to teach Jack to clean his room. Which of the two lists below is the better analysis of the job?

41

a. List 1:
1. Pick up things.
2. Make the bed.
3. Clean the floor and furniture.
4. Close the closet doors.

b. List 2:
1. Put all toys in toy box.
2. Put dirty clothes in hamper.
3. Dust the floor with dust mop.
4. Dust the bed, dresser, chair, and toy box.
5. Make the bed.
6. Replace any furniture that has been moved. (Marks on the floor are handy for this.)
7. Close dresser drawers and closet doors.
8. Turn out light.

To repeat, it is wise not to comment on the finished product unless he asks you. In that case, say "It's fine," and do not mention minor flaws. He will correct them as he becomes more skillful. If he has failed to perform a whole step, simply say "You haven't finished," and leave so that he can complete his work.

42 | After Mother made the list, she started the plan described earlier, letting Jack do an increasing number of steps. On the ninth day Jack did the chore by himself. He called Mother to inspect his work. Mother looked around and saw that he had done a pretty good job, but the bedspread was on upside down, a fire truck protruded from the toy box, and the lamp shade was askew. Which remark should she make?
   a. "That's fine."
   b. "Pretty good, but what about that lamp shade? And the bedspread is upside down, you know."

43 | On the eleventh day Jack called Mother to inspect again. This time the bedspread was on correctly, though somewhat wrinkled. The closet doors were open. Which remark should Mother make?
   a. "The closet doors are open."
   b. "You haven't finished."

44 | A few minutes later Jack called Mother again, saying "How is it now?" The doors were shut, and the bedspread was still wrinkled. What should she say?
   a. "That's fine."
   b. "You haven't finished."

Choosing an Enforceable Rule

Whenever Mother states a rule, she should anticipate that the rule will be broken. As discussed earlier, a healthy, normal child needs to test any rule that makes a difference in his life. The parent, then, must be certain that she can enforce the rule consistently. If she cannot enforce it, she cannot expect the child to follow it.

The answer to one question will help you establish whether a rule is enforceable:

**Will you know every time the child breaks the rule,
without depending on other people's testimony?**

In each item below, circle the rule that is enforceable from this standpoint. (Assume the parent is at home most of the time, unless otherwise stated.)

45
a. "Jack, do the dishes before bedtime every Thursday night."
b. "Jack, don't hit your brother any more."

46
a. "Mabel, be sure to wash your hands before you eat lunch at school."
b. "Mabel, be sure to wash your hands before you come to the dinner table."

47
a. "Joseph, you must change your school clothes before you go out to play."
b. "Joseph, I want you to go easy on that sore leg. Don't do any running for three days."

48 | a. Danny's mother works from 9 to 5. Danny gets out of school at 3:00. "Danny, I want you to come directly home from school every day and change your clothes. No playing until you do."
b. "Danny, the trash must be emptied every day before I get home."

49 | a. Martha is three. Her mother is very busy keeping house and looking after a baby brother. Martha has learned to climb over the fence. "Martha, you must stay in the yard. Don't climb over the fence."
b. "Martha, I don't want you running in and out. Stay outside until I call you."

50 | a. "Jo Ann, you may not wear lipstick at school until you are fifteen."
b. "Jo Ann, your skirts must reach your knees."

A parent, then, must be able to find out easily whether a rule has been broken. In addition, the parent must have a plan of enforcement to use whenever the rule is broken. The next section of this program will deal with the question "How are rules enforced?"

51 | *Criterion Frame*
Think of an example of a definable, reasonable, and enforceable rule. Write it as you would say it to the child.

ENFORCING A RULE

ENFORCEMENT OF "CHORE RULES"

There are 3 steps in the enforcement of most rules. They are: (1) set a time limit; (2) ensure that the task is carried out; and (3) ignore irrelevant behavior.

Step 1: Set A Time Limit

The first step in enforcing a rule is to set a time limit (instances where this is not possible will be discussed later). When a rule requires the performance of some task, the parent must specify when the task has to be done. The end of the time limit is an *event* in which the child usually participates. For example, John must make his bed *before he leaves for school* (event); Marie must do the dishes *before she goes to bed* (event).

Which of the following rules has the more specific time limit? (Circle one in each item.)

52   a. Belle must mow the grass before she eats supper.
      b. Belle must mow the grass pretty soon.

53   a. Leon must do the vacuuming after school.
      b. Leon must do the vacuuming before he goes out to play.

54   a. Hank must practice piano for a half hour before he can watch TV.
      b. Hank must practice piano for a half hour every day, or he cannot watch TV for a week.

55   a. Walter must cut the grass by lunch time on Saturday.
      b. Walter must cut the grass once a week or he is "grounded" (confined to the house) for 10 days.

Step 2: Ensure That the Task is Carried Out

The second step in enforcing a rule of this sort is to ensure that the task is carried out. When an event signals the end of the time limit (like bedtime or supper time), the parent must prevent the child from participating in the event until the task is completed. The following examples show how this is accomplished.

Case 1

Belle came in for supper. She had not finished mowing the lawn. Father said "You must mow the lawn before supper."

"I'll finish it after supper," Belle replied, sitting down.

Father said "You must mow the lawn before supper."

At this point Belle refused to finish the task. Father removed Belle's plate and glass. Belle sat at the table for 15 minutes alternating verbal tantrums with periods of sullen silence. The family ignored her outbursts, acting as if she were not there. Finally Belle got up and finished her job.

Case 2

Marie went to bed without doing the dishes. As soon as Mother discovered this, she went into Marie's room, turned on the light, and said "The rule is that the dishes must be done before you go to bed."

Marie turned over, pretending to be asleep.

Mother said nothing more. She merely stood there, waiting. After 2 minutes, Marie started to mutter angrily. Mother remained waiting quietly. After 3 more minutes, Marie got out of bed and trudged to the kitchen. Mother went to her own room, saying nothing more.

Case 3

Hank, an inveterate TV fan, did not practice piano on Wednesday. After dinner he went downstairs and turned on the TV. Dad came down after him and turned it off, saying "What's the rule?"

Hank replied morosely "No piano, no TV." He sat down sullenly. Dad went back upstairs. A few minutes later Hank turned on the TV, very softly. Dad, aware of this possibility, came down again in a few minutes, bringing the newspaper. Saying nothing, he turned off the TV and sat down to read. Hank sat quietly for a half hour. Then he went to bed.

The next day, Hank did not practice again. He waited until Dad's favorite TV program was on, then turned on the set. Dad came downstairs and said "You know the rule. You will have to leave." Hank went upstairs and practiced, joining Dad for the last half of the program.

Case 4

Leon vacuumed all of the room and went out to play. But he neglected to replace the furniture which had been specified as part of the job. Mom called but received no response. She searched the neighborhood and finally found him. Mom said "You haven't finished your job." Leon refused to come home. Mom picked him up and carried him. Halfway home, Leon asked to walk.

When he got home, he hurriedly replaced all the furniture except one chair, and ran outside. Mom followed him, caught him, and carried him back. Leon replaced the chair.

Two cases are described below. Circle the one in which the parent enforces the rule.

56

a. John has to make his bed before he goes to school. The school bus is due in 2 minutes. John hurries out the door. Mom catches him and repeats the rule. John has a tantrum and the bus leaves without him. Mother keeps John inside, but does not limit him in other ways. At noon his bed is still not made. He stays home.

b. John has not made his bed and the school bus is coming. Mom keeps him home. At noon, he still has not made the bed. An important test is coming up, so she sends him to school, but tells him "No TV for a week."

57

a. The rule is that Julie (age 2) must go to her playroom when she leaves the dinner table. Julie has not been feeling well and ate very little supper. When she left the table, she wandered into the kitchen. Dad said "The playroom, Julie." She remained in the kitchen. Dad started to stand up. Julie ran back to the table, got up in her chair, and ate a bite of potatoes. Then she got down and ran into the kitchen. Dad stood up. Julie ran back to the table.

b. Julie, not feeling well, left the table after only a few bites of food. She wandered into the kitchen. Dad said "The playroom, Julie." Julie did not respond. Dad stood up. Julie ran back to the table. Dad carried her downstairs. She screamed "I wanna eat. Hungry, Dad, I wanna eat." Dad said nothing, put her in the playroom, and closed the gate.

In the following situations, what would you do? (Circle *a* or *b*.)

58 | *Rule:*
Billy must wash his face and hands before dinner.

Situation:
Billy comes to the table without washing.
You say "Billy, you must wash before dinner."
Bill ways "Aw, gee whiz! I washed when I came in an hour ago. I haven't done anything since then."

Alternative responses:
a. Say "You must wash before dinner."
b. Say "Well, all right, as long as it was just an hour ago."

59 | *Rule:*
Mike must change his school clothes and shoes before going out to play.

Situation:
Mike changed his shirt and pants but not his shoes. He is a half mile away at his boy friend's home.

Alternative responses:
a. Let it go this time since he is so far away.
b. Telephone the friend and speak to Mike, saying "Mike, you have to change your shoes before going out."

60 | *Situation:*
You telephone Mike; 20 minutes later he has not appeared.

Alternative responses:
a. When he comes home for dinner, tell him that he has lost his TV privileges for the evening.
b. Go out and find him. Bring him home to change his shoes, carrying him if necessary.

A rule which is not enforced is far more damaging than no rule at all. If you are *unwilling* to enforce it, it is an unenforceable rule.

61

Rule:

Carolyn must do the dishes before going to bed.

Situation:

It is a new rule, and Carolyn is testing. It is 11:30 and the dishes are not done. Carolyn is reading a book. You have not said anything to her about the dishes. You are ready for bed.

Alternatives:

a. Insist that she come to bed now, and do the dishes before she goes to school the next morning.

b. Say "The dishes must be done before you go to bed, Carolyn." Then go to bed.

62

Criterion Frame

Rule:

Wendy must baby-sit with her baby brother on the first and third Thursday nights of every month. Any changes in this arrangement have to be cleared a week in advance.

Situation:

Wendy "forgot" and accepted a date for the first Thursday. She also forgot to tell her mother until Wednesday. "But Mom," she says, "can't you change your plans to Friday? You aren't doing anything special. And I have been waiting for this boy to ask me all year."

What should you do?

Step 3: Ignore Irrelevant Behavior

When a parent enforces a new rule, she changes the environment in several ways. She is acting differently, the child is acting differently, and often the home appears different to the child as a result of the action. It is not surprising, then, that a child becomes upset. He must test the rule to see if it will stand. He must test you to see if you are consistent. He tests by breaking the rule, by breaking a part of the rule, by arguing, by pleading, by having a temper tantrum, by providing you with a reasonable excuse for not enforcing the rule.

All of these behaviors are necessary and important for the learning process. They are, however, irrelevant to the task to be performed. Therefore, they must be ignored.

Why Should You Ignore Irrelevant Behavior?

The most powerful technique for eliminating many behaviors is to ignore them. This may sound unbelievable to parents who spend a great deal of time praising a child when he does something right and punishing him when he does something wrong. You may have observed this principle in action, however. A small child hears his parents say "Thank you" and "You're welcome" to each other. He begins saying "Thank you" at various times. If his parents ignore his effort, that is, do not respond with "You're welcome," he will soon stop saying "Thank you."

Here is another example. A mother had "tried everything" to keep her 2-year-old from climbing into the baby's buggy. First she tried to distract the child by interesting her in other activities. Then, for a week, she spanked her every time it happened. Finally, in desperation, she decided to give up. As long as the baby wasn't in the buggy, she would ignore the 2-year-old when she climbed in. After two weeks the child rarely climbed in the buggy.

A teacher decided that her students had developed a habit of raising their hands for help when it was not necessary. She stopped responding to hand-raising. She did not smile or frown or otherwise notice students who raised their hands. She continued whatever she was doing. After the first week, they stopped raising their hands. (The quality of their work indicated that the teacher was right in assuming they did not need help.)

In order to eliminate the tears and tantrums, arguments and appeals, reasons and recriminations that will accompany the enforcement of a new rule, the parent must *not* respond to these irrelevant behaviors.

Which of the behaviors below should be ignored? (Circle *a* or *b*.)

---

63   a. Johnny kicks and screams when Father insists that he change his clothes before going out.

        b. Johnny slips out without changing his clothes.

---

64   a. Mary Lou forgets to wash one of the windows that is included in her chore.

        b. Mary Lou calls her mother a "nasty old witch" when she insists the job be finished.

---

65   a. Brad holds his breath until he turns blue after he has been told he must pick up his toys.

        b. Brad picks up only half of his toys before coming to dinner.

---

66   a. When told she can't go out until her room is clean, Inez runs to her room, slams the door, and throws the contents of her dresser and closet on the floor.

        b. Inez piles all the contents of her drawers into the closet and shuts the door, although the rule states that clothes must be put away.

Which of the behaviors below should be ignored? (Circle *a* or *b*.)

67
a. Diane is in a big hurry because her date is due shortly. She puts the pans in the oven without washing them.
b. Diane says "Please let me do the dishes tomorrow night, instead. I didn't know my school meeting would last so long. I won't have time to change before my date gets here. Or at least let me do them when I get home. Just this once won't hurt."

68
a. George neglects to empty the trash.
b. George says "Dad, it's silly to empty the trash tonight. The baskets are only half full."

69
a. Gordon complains of a stomachache and sore foot after dinner.
b. Gordon goes to bed without doing the dishes.

How Do You Ignore Behaviors?

It is not surprising that parents find it difficult, at first, to ignore irrelevant behaviors. They ask "How can you ignore a kicking, screaming child?" "How can you allow a child to call you names and use vile language?" "How can you fail to answer a child's arguments—especially when you have good answers?"

It *is* difficult at first, but with practice it becomes quite easy. When a child performs an irrelevant behavior, you do not respond. You do not smile, frown, console, berate, answer, spank, distract, or ridicule. As far as you are concerned, the behavior did not occur. You did not see it or hear it. You concentrate solely on going about your business (if necessary, invent some business). If the behavior is extremely upsetting to you, you may find it easier to go to another part of the house, or out for a walk. If this is necessary, do it slowly and calmly. (Hurrying out of the room is a very definite response.)

In the following cases, what should you do? (Circle *a* or *b*.)

| 70 | Gary is crying and hitting his head against the wall. |

    a. Continue reading the newspaper.

    b. Give him his favorite teddy bear and some other toys.

| 71 | Marlene has just called you a "damn, stinking bastard." |

    a. Say "If you ever speak to me like that again, I will take you over my knee, no matter how big you are."

    b. Drink your coffee.

| 72 | Pat says "I don't know why I have to do the dishes. None of my friends do. Most of them don't have any chores at all." |

    a. Do not answer. Scratch the dog's belly.

    b. Say "What your friends' parents do is their business, not mine. If you don't have any chores, you will never learn responsibility."

73 | Judy is having a tantrum because the **TV** program she wanted to watch is not on tonight.
a. Go into the kitchen and have a peanut butter sandwich.
b. Switch the dial to all the channels to prove that the program is not on.

74 | William just complained of a stomachache. (It is time for him to feed the dog.)
a. Smile a small private smile.
b. Continue making dinner.

75 | Winona, in a bad temper, broke one of your favorite vases while doing the dusting.
a. Give her a well-deserved spanking.
b. Suppress your tears, say nothing, and later remove breakable items from the room temporarily.

There remain two important points with regard to irrelevant behavior.

1. Although a great deal of anger may seem to be directed at you, it should not be regarded as a "personal attack." The child is using you to help him eliminate some unrealistic expectations. He has to express his anger and upsetness, and you happen to be there at the right time. He really does not want you to notice his behavior. One indication of this "need to be ignored" is that comforting a child in this condition seems to make it worse. He gets over the tantrum more quickly and feels better about it if you just leave him alone.

2. There is only one exception to the rule of ignoring irrelevant behavior. If a child strikes you, leave the situation as calmly and quickly as possible, without commenting. It is very seldom that a child will lose control of himself to this extent, even in a tantrum. (This behavior is not uncommon with very young children, of course. Two- and three-year-olds should be handled in the same way.)

ENFORCEMENT OF "PROBLEM RULES"

Most rules can be set up so that something must be done by a certain time. Sometimes, however, parents find it necessary to establish rules which do not have time limits. These rules are usually designed to solve some problem that has arisen. For example, Bob has the habit of taking off his shoes and leaving them in the living room. Betty has been coming home very late from her dates. Peter never washes the tub after taking a bath. Jake has a habit of cursing whenever he talks. In these cases, a parent might establish rules such as:

"Bob's shoes must be put in his room when he takes them off."

"Betty must be home by 12:00."

"The tub must be cleaned after every bath."

"No swearing."

"Chore rules" are set up to make the environment more consistent and comfortable. However, rules like the ones above should be established *only* when a problem exists and steadfast ignoring of the situation has not eliminated the behavior. (Allow a week or so and, if no improvement is evident, a rule may be necessary.)

Like "chore rules," the rule must be definable, reasonable, and enforceable. The enforcement routine, however, differs slightly from the one described in the last section. The behaviors covered by these rules may occur often and at unpredictable times. A time limit is not useful in enforcing them. For example, to say "Bob must take his shoes to his room before dinner" does not solve the problem. Mother doesn't want the shoes in the living room at any time. Peter takes a bath at different times, sometimes before supper, sometimes after supper, sometimes in the morning (sometimes not at all). Having him clean the tub before he goes to bed does not help the person who takes a bath after Peter is through.

Rules like "No swearing" and "Be home by 12:00" do not concern tasks at all so no time limit is possible. When they are broken, the situation cannot be undone or corrected.

Which of the rules below is a "problem rule," rather than a "chore rule." (Circle *a* or *b*.)

| 76 | a. Wash the dishes on Thursday night before bedtime.
b. Hang up your coat when you take it off. |

| 77 | a. Turn off the lights when leaving an empty **room**.
b. Make your bed before you leave for school. |

| 78 | a. Don't slide down the bannister.
b. Sweep the steps every afternoon before you go out to play. |

Enforcement of "problem rules" has two steps: (1) ask for a restatement of the rule; and (2) ignore irrelevant behavior.

Step 1: Restate the Rule

Whenever a child breaks the rule, restate the rule (unemotionally). This procedure sounds so simple that it is hard to believe it could be effective. However, we have used this method with classes of normal and problem children, and have worked with parents who have problems with their children. Our experience indicates that it is more effective and easier to use than any system of punishments and penalties.

If the rule covers a situation that can be corrected (like leaving shoes in the living room), then the parent must ensure that the child corrects his mistake. The procedure here is the same as ensuring that a child carries out a chore (see page 34). If the situation cannot be corrected (like coming home after the curfew), a restatement of the rule is sufficient.

Several situations are described below. Which response is appropriate with regard to this method of enforcement?

---

79 | *Rule:*
No reading in bed after 10:30.

Situation:
Marlene is reading in bed. It is 10:45.

Alternative responses:
a. Open the door and say "Marlene, if I catch you breaking this rule once more, you will be grounded for a week."
b. Open the door and say "The rule is no reading after 10:30." Wait until the light is off before leaving.

---

80 | *Rule:*
Rinse and hang up your bathing suit and towel after swimming.

Situation:
Gale has left his swimming trunks and towel in a damp heap on the bathroom floor.

Alternatives:
a. Find Gale and say "The rule is rinse and hang up swimming gear."
b. Pick them up and hang them on the line since company is due any minute. Later tell Gale "You broke the rule."

---

81 | *Rule:*
Speak German at the dinner table.

Situation:
(Herman's parents are concerned that he is losing his ability to speak a second language so they have established this rule.) Herman says "Pass the salt, please."

Alternatives.
a. Say "You know how important it is that you use your German. Why can't you cooperate?"
b. Say "Die Regel ist, wir sprechen Deutsch am Tisch." (Translation: The rule is, we speak German at the table.)

---

82 | *Rule:*
Be home by 12:00.

Situation:
Elaine walks in at 12:30.

Alternatives:
a. Say "I've had enough. This is the third night in a row you have been late. You could have telephoned at least. No more dates for a month."
b. Say "The rule is be home by 12:00."

Step 2: Ignore Irrelevant Behavior

Enforcement of rules by this method will be followed by the same kinds of irrelevant behaviors that have been described earlier (see page 40). These behaviors should be ignored in the way that has been specified on pages 44-47 of this program.

Special Case: Enforcement by Establishing Routines

Some problems can be solved by establishing routines which are consistently followed. Like "problem rules," parents set these up only after a problem arises that has not been solved by ignoring it. One example concerns Warren who was always late for dinner. His mother established a rule for herself: "Dinner will be served at 6:00." If Warren wasn't there, the family went ahead. When he arrived, dinner was cold or all gone. (If it was gone, Mother allowed him to fix himself a bowl of corn flakes and a glass of milk.) After a few days of testing, Warren was seldom late for dinner.

Another problem was Kristin, who had to be called for dinner a dozen times. Kristin's mother could not set a precise hour for dinner since Dad worked irregular hours. Instead she told Kristin that, from now on, she would call her only once. They would sit down to eat exactly five minutes after that. Kristin tested the rule for a few days, but after three dinners of corn flakes she began arriving on time. Kristin's mother was pleased to find that this behavior carried over, and Kristin had to be called only once at other times.

Several problems are described below. Choose the routine which would solve the problem.

---

83 | *Problem:*
Amanda will not get up in the morning.

Alternatives:
a. Call Amanda only once (be certain she responds), 45 minutes before she must leave for school.
b. Cut out TV privileges for any day that Amanda has to be called more than once.

---

84 | *Problem:*
Quentin (age 8) is never ready to leave for church on time.

Alternatives:
a. Dress him yourself to be sure he is ready.
b. Tell him the time 15 minutes before you will leave. If he is not ready, leave without him.

---

85 | *Criterion Frame*
Problem:
In spite of his mother's constant nagging, Desmond is always late for school.

Suggest a rotuine that would solve this problem.

ENFORCEMENT OF COMMANDS

When a parent issues a command like "Don't go out yet," or "Tie your shoes," or "You've had enough ice cream," he is obligated to enforce it in the same way that he enforces long-term rules. He sets a time limit if he can. He ensures that the task is carried out if there is a task. If there is no task, he restates the command which has been violated. He ignores irrelevant behavior.

If a parent counted the commands he usually gives in a day, the number would probably astound him. Enforcing the small proportion of these commands that can be enforced requires more time and energy than most parents possess. The moral of the story: "Issue as few commands as possible." Let the child find out for himself the consequences of his act whenever possible. This point will be discussed more fully in the section "Natural Consequences of Behaviors," page 81.

A child of 4 or 5 is capable of carrying out some simple "chore rule." This makes a small corner of his life stable and secure. Whenever he is frightened, he can test his parent's consistency with regard to the chore rule. A child who does not have a chore, however, has no focus for his testing. He tests many of the commands given by his parents. And he usually finds that his parents are not consistent. It is especially important, then, for parents of very young children to enforce commands consistently and to uphold all routines. It is the only way a parent can stabilize a corner of the child's life. It frees the child to notice other things around him, at a time when this learning is crucial.

In the cases below, what would you do? (Circle *a* or *b*.)

86 | Belle asks for a cookie, but it is too near dinner time. You say "No cookie now." Belle screams and stamps her feet.
 a. Say nothing.
 b. Give her a cookie to keep her quiet.

87 | Ozzie wants to go outside. You say "Put your jacket on first." Ozzie says "No, I don't want to wear a jacket." When you try to put it on him, he fights.
 a. Say "Okay, go on without it. You'll see how cold it is."
 b. Wait until the tantrum is over, and put on his jacket before he goes out.

88 | Philip is going to visit his friend. You say "Be home by 6:00 because we are going out for dinner. If you aren't here, we will go without you." At 6:00 Philip is not home.
 a. Go without him.
 b. Call and ask the friend's mother to send him home.

89 | Jean asks if she can wear your gloves when she goes out on her date. You say "No, I need them myself." As she is leaving, you notice she is wearing the gloves.
 a. Say nothing since she would be embarrassed.
 b. Say "What did I say about the gloves?"

RESULTS OF CONSISTENCY TRAINING

THE IMPORTANCE
OF STARTING WITH ONLY ONE RULE

You will be tempted to "wipe the slate clean" by setting up rules to handle all existing problems. Yielding to this temptation would be unwise. Begin with only *one* well-defined, clearly enforceable rule.

There are several reasons for starting with one rule. *First,* if the parent has been inconsistent in the past, the child's testing of the first rule will be more extreme and last longer than it will for later rules. The enforcement of this rule will require all the energy you can muster. The first rule establishes your consistency. When the child learns that you will act consistently in enforcing one rule, he will conclude, with less testing, that you will be consistent in enforcing another rule.

Second, every rule changes a child's environment. It is going to be very hard for him to get used to one change. If he must get used to several changes, it may be overwhelming for him.

Third, parents have found that, when one rule is established, a child aims all his rebellion at that one rule. He abandons many of his other misbehaviors and concentrates on breaking that one rule to the best of his ability. This is useful to the parent who has a clear enforcement plan. She knows exactly what to do when the child breaks the rule, and she can handle irrelevant behaviors. An example of this occurred in a classroom where a teacher established only one rule: "No talking." Other behaviors, like throwing paper wads, passing notes, popping gum, etc., were quickly eliminated when the teacher ignored them. He responded only when a child talked by saying to him "What's the rule?" Immediately there were many more instances of talking. Also, the children tried all varieties of talking—whispering, shouting, reading aloud, singing. Within 10 days, there was practically no talking. But, whenever a child felt a need to test the teacher, he did it by talking rather than by poking his neighbor or by dropping his pencil. One advantage, then, of having only one rule is that the testing behaviors are channeled into the testing of one rule. The parent can devise a plan for handling the testing behaviors.

A *fourth* reason for starting with one rule is that a child cannot remember more than one rule at a time. As one parent said "I recall when I was learning to drive that I was given several rules to follow when shifting gears. 'Take your foot off the accelerator before you push in the clutch.' 'Push in the clutch before you shift.' 'Press on the accelerator before you let the clutch up.' 'Don't press so much!' and many more. I usually felt accomplished if I remembered to do one thing correctly. It was months before I could do them all." A child would feel as bewildered as this parent if she were told: "Empty the trash every night before dinner. Hang up your coat when you take it off. Wash out the tub after a bath. And dinner will be at six o'clock every night."

Finally, you will discover that things change around the house after the enforcement of just one rule. Many of the rules that seem necessary now apply to problems that may clear up in several weeks. Other problems may arise instead. So give your child and yourself a chance to adjust to a new situation. After establishing one "chore rule," add another rule only when a serious problem arises.

Which of the parents below will probably be more successful in enforcing the rules?

90
a. Mr. Brown has posted a list of 10 regulations for his son to observe when using the workshop.
b. Mr. Jones tells his son "When you are finished in the workshop, replace the tools in their proper holders."

91
a. Mrs. Johnson tells her daughter: "From now on you will clean your room on Wednesday afternoon before dinner."
b. Mrs. Jackson tells her daugher: "Things are going to be different around here. You will clean your room before dinner on Wednesday. You will be called only once in the morning. Dinner will be served at 6:30, and you have the responsibility for getting there on time. And phone calls are limited to 3 minutes."

WHICH BEHAVIORS SHOULD YOU EXPECT?

The extent of testing a rule and the extremity of irrelevant behaviors will be different for each child. Without exception, however, a child's behavior will "get worse before it gets better." Many older children seem to regress to a 2-year-old level, indulging in good old-fashioned temper tantrums. Children who express anger easily and often will express even more anger during the crucial period after a new rule is established. Parents of these children will probably be less shocked, however, than the parents of shy, withdrawn children, or the parents of amiable, easy-going children. The extent of the violence just under the surface in these children is likely to be very upsetting to their parents. It is necessary, however, for such children to be allowed to express their anger without interference. Their expectations will be more realistic as a result.

A common pattern is found in a child's testing of a new rule (your experience may not be as extreme as this, but it is best to be prepared for the worst). In the following description, assume that a daily chore has been assigned. If a chore is to be done weekly, or twice weekly, the amount of time necessary for each phase will be longer.

On the first day or two things may go very smoothly, and the rule will be carried out with a minimum of enforcement by the parents. This phase is followed by a sharp rise in testing behaviors. The child will break the rule in every way imaginable. The number of irrelevant behaviors will increase, and the child will become very emotional. This second phase may last several days. It is at this time that parents usually back down on the enforcement of a rule. They are upset by the child's extreme behavior. Enforcing the rule seems more trouble than it's worth. Instead of getting better, things get worse. Hold on, however, for if a parent is consistent through this phase, the testing diminishes. The irrelevant behaviors drop away. The child seems happier and more relaxed. The parent heaves a sigh of relief. But too soon it seems! In about a week there is a relapse. This is less extreme than the first testing, but it is upsetting to parents. "Are we going to go through *that* again?" they wonder. This testing period is over quickly, however, and testing practically disappears. There are few, if any, irrelevant behaviors. Life seems easier than before.

Some cases are described below. You will see this pattern operating.

Case 1

Rule: Miles must make his bed before going to school. (Miles must be at school at 8:30. He must leave by 8:25. He gets up at 7:30.)

Day 1

Miles makes his bed at 8:10. Leaves at 8:20.

Day 2

Miles makes his bed at 8:00, but leaves pillow on floor. Starts to leave at 8:20. Mother says "You haven't finished your job." Miles argues. Mother says nothing. He finishes the job. Leaves at 8:26.

Day 3

Miles gets up late. Attempts to leave at 8:25 without making bed. Mother stops him. He argues and cries. He makes his bed at 8:34. Leaves for school at 8:39.

Day 4

Miles dawdles all morning. At 8:25 he tries to leave without making his bed. When Mother stops him, he flies into a rage, kicking and screaming, using abusive language. At 8:45 he goes to his room. At 8:55 he leaves for school, his bed made.

Day 5

At breakfast Miles says he doesn't think he can make his bed today because he has a sore hand. He can't close it. He drops a spoon to prove it. Mother says nothing. Muttering to himself, he makes his bed at 8:05. Leaves at 8:25.

Day 6
Miles makes his bed at 8:10. Leaves at 8:25.

Day 7
Miles makes his bed at 7:45, before breakfast. Comments that it is a lot easier when you don't have to worry about it all through breakfast.

Days 8-16
Few problems. Miles usually makes his bed before breakfast.

Day 17
Miles gets up late. Tries to leave without making his bed. Mother stops him and he argues briefly. Makes his bed and leaves at 8:30.

Day 18
Miles leaves his bed pulled out into the center of the room. Tries to leave at 8:15. Mother stops him. He cries and stamps his feet. At 8:25 he pushes the bed back. Leaves at 8:27.

Days 19-30
Miles makes his bed before breakfast.

Mother made 2 charts of Miles' behaviors during this time.

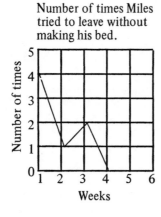

Number of times Miles tried to leave without making his bed.

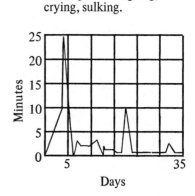

Time spent in arguing, crying, sulking.

Case 2

Problem: Martha has discovered the doorbell. She rings it numerous times during the day. This has become a nuisance. Mother decides to eliminate the behavior by ignoring the bell. Below is a chart of the number of times Martha rang the bell each day.

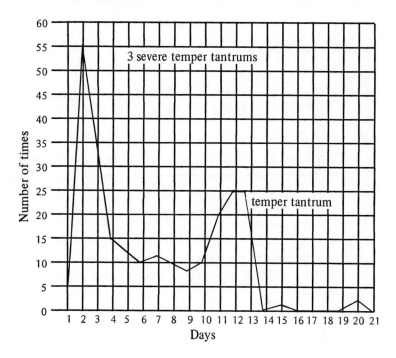

Case 3

Problem: At dinner Louis leaves the table to play, then comes back and resumes eating. This happens 5 to 6 times during a meal.

Rule: Parents remove his plate after he leaves the first time.

Day 1
Louis does not get down until he is finished.

Day 2
Louis gets down. He comes back to find his plate gone. He becomes very angry, cries, kicks, attempts to hit baby sister. Mother removes sister.

Day 3
Louis gets down. He comes back to find his plate gone. He argues that he thought he was through, but now he is hungry again. When parents do not respond, he cries.

Day 4
Louis gets down. He comes back to find his plate gone. He becomes very angry. He announces "I'm going to put my fist through that window if you don't give me some food." He puts his fist through the window. The cuts are bandaged.

Day 5
Louis does not get down until finished.

Day 6-9
Louis carries his plate to the kitchen when finished.

Day 10
Louis gets down. He comes back in a few minutes, and his plate is gone. He says nothing and leaves the room.

Below is a chart of the time spent each day in temper tantrums.

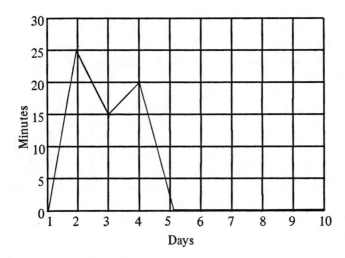

Because so many parents abandon a rule when a child tests it, we have been careful to prepare parents for this unpleasant period. If you know what to expect, it will not be so upsetting when it happens. If you know why a child needs to test rules, you will not regard his anger as a personal attack. We should emphasize, however, that this testing period is temporary and relatively brief. If you are consistent, a child will need to test the rule only a few times. The irrelevant behaviors will drop away very rapidly if they are ignored. It may be helpful to keep a chart like those above. It is easy, today, to forget how bad things were yesterday. A chart can help to keep things in perspective, and will point out the progress which is made.

92 Joyce and Royce present the same problems to their parents. They are both usually late for dinner. Below is a chart of the number of minutes each child was late for dinner for 10 days. Which chart indicates that the parents used consistency training techniques, as described in this program?

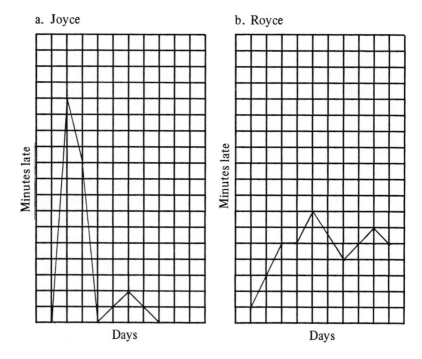

a. Joyce

b. Royce

93 Hank and Frank have started swearing commonly around the house. Each household has instituted the rule "No swearing." Look at the charts below and decide which parents are enforcing the rule consistently.

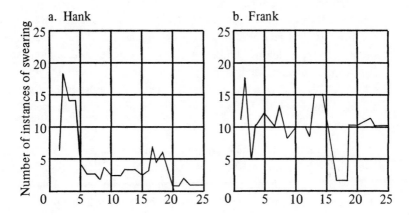

a. Hank   b. Frank

Number of instances of swearing

WHAT HAPPENS TO THE PARENT?

It seems as though life should be much more comfortable for a parent after a child stops testing a new rule. Very often a long-standing battle has been resolved, and the child is at last behaving as you want him to. Unfortunately, it isn't quite that easy. In the long run, life *will* seem more comfortable. But *you* have to get used to things first. Adults react to new situations very much as children do. They are upset and anxious when they cannot predict what is likely to happen. As a result of your consistency, the child is acting differently. Thus, you must re-learn what to expect from the child. Below is a description of what may happen to you after you successfully establish a rule.

First, after establishing a new rule, you may see a lot of things about your child's behavior that you never noticed before. You will find that his actions are much more reasonable than they seemed before. This can be a very exciting experience, and you will probably want to tell people about it—your spouse, neighbors, and friends.

But after a while you may notice that you become angry or fearful with very little cause. Sometimes there doesn't seem to be any cause at all. This is an adult equivalent of a temper tantrum. You are reacting to the change in your child. After you get to know him again, these moods will subside. Knowing that these moods are natural and normal should make them easier to bear.

Finally, other members of the family are likely to react to the change in you and the child. Temper tantrums, arguments, verbal attacks, etc., are a temporary result. If these can be ignored, a new equilibrium can be established more quickly.

Several situations are described below. Choose the interpretation which is based on the preceding discussion.

94 | Your child has stopped testing the rule. He carries out his chore routinely. You find that numerous things he does are annoying to you. He slouches at the table. His face is usually dirty. He forgets to say "Thank you." Yet none of these things used to bother you.
- a. You never realized before what an obnoxious child he is.
- b. Your anger is the result of the child's acting differently. You don't know what to expect.

95 | Betty now does the dishes without being told. She seems more relaxed and better-natured. But now you are having trouble with brother Jimmy. He seems to do everything to annoy you.
- a. You and Jimmy are both temporarily upset by the change in Betty.
- b. Jimmy is just trying to get attention.

96 | Things seemed so much better after you established a consistent dinner time. They still are. But you find that several times a day you have black moods when you just want to pound something or yell. These moods are usually followed by periods of anxiety, when you feel as though you can't move. Your heart beats faster and you perspire.
- a. You are going crazy.
- b. This is a temporary reaction to the change in the routine and the change in everybody's behavior.

97 | Your child has stopped testing the rule, and the discomfort of getting used to his new behaviors is over for you. Lately your spouse seems to be picking fights. Nothing you do is right.
   a. Your spouse doesn't love you any more.
   b. Your spouse is reacting to the change in you and in the child. He is upset, doesn't know why, and is trying to find a reason to be upset.

In the cases below, which action would be based on the principles of this program?

98 | You are feeling angry and "on edge." You suspect this is a result of changes in your son's behavior.
   a. Visit your mother, who has been sick lately.
   b. Find a good hard job to do, and "work off" your anger. Stay away from people.

99 | You find yourself in the middle of a silly argument with your daughter. You realize that you aren't really angry with *her*. It is your son's new behavior that is upsetting.
   a. Withdraw from the argument and wash some walls.
   b. Start an argument with your son.

100 | Your husband is criticizing your housekeeping, and you just finished a thorough spring cleaning. You realize that he is getting used to the change in yourself and your child.
- a. Since his criticism is an "irrelevant behavior," ignore it and continue making dinner.
- b. Cry, and point out how unfair and unjust his criticism is.

101 | Your wife is upset by the changes in you and your daughter, although she probably doesn't know *why* she is upset. Her "temper tantrum" consists of nagging at you all weekend to do little household jobs.
- a. Since nagging is an "irrelevant behavior," ignore it and do what you want to do.
- b. Do the jobs to try to keep her happy.

If in doubt about this item, see (1) on page 47.

3

CREATING A
COMFORTABLE ENVIRONMENT

A parent's job is to create an environment in which his child can grow. Although parents will agree with this statement, they often act as though their main job were to prevent bad habits and instill good ones. They fill the child's life with ineffective warnings and "good advice." The child is seldom free to discover the natural consequences of his actions. If, instead, a parent concentrated his efforts on making the whole environment safe for exploration and free from unnecessary tension, both parents and child would be happier and more successful.

In which case below is the parent interested primarily in "creating an environment" rather than controlling a particular behavior?

| 102 | a. Mother puts nourishing food on the table. |
| | b. Mother insists that Richard finish his spinach. |

| 103 | a. Millie's parents provide her with attractive clothes. |
| | b. Millie's mother tells her what she should wear. |

| 104 | a. Dad insists that Calvin spend 45 minutes every night on his science homework. |
| | b. Dad takes Calvin to the zoo when he asks to go. |

| 105 | a. Mom requires Belinda to do the dishes whenever she is too tired to do them herself. |
| | b. Mom requires Belinda to do the dishes every Thursday because she knows that Belinda needs the consistency that the rule provides. |

An environment which allows a child to develop his potential has three characteristics:

1. *limits* (or rules, already discussed);
2. *freedom* to discover things "by myself"; and
3. *a model* (a person who provides a pattern for the child).

This program has dealt extensively with limits or rules. The other characteristics, a model and freedom to discover, are just as necessary for normal development. The parent as model is discussed in relation to moral training (page 99). The following section deals with freedom to discover.

Providing Freedom to Discover

Listen in at Mrs. Johnson's house as she talks to her 3-year-old: "Don't touch that plug—you'll get a shock." "Don't climb on that chair—you'll fall." "You have to eat your lunch or you'll be hungry in an hour." "Don't put that in your mouth—it tastes awful."

She talks to her 10-year-old: "Don't ride your bike no-handed—you'll break your neck." "If you don't learn to share, no one will play with you." "Don't gulp your food—you'll get a stomachache."

She talks to her 15-year-old: "You can't do your best without a good breakfast." "Hurry or you'll be late." "It would be much easier to keep your room clean if you would only put your clothes away instead of throwing them on the floor."

An observer would notice two things about this mother's attempt to "guide and advise" her children. First, she is surprisingly ineffective. She says the same thing day after day. Her children behave the same way day after day. Second, much of her advice isn't true. The 3-year-old continues to climb and seldom falls. The 10-year-old has many friends, though he appears to be as selfish as ever. The 15-year-old gets good grades and never manages more than a glass of juice for breakfast.

Why is it that parents continue to engage in such a frustrating and ineffective activity? Perhaps parents feel responsible for what their child does and the impression the child makes on other people. Yet they know that they have very limited control of the child's behavior. Furthermore, they are fearful of what will happen to the child, and they feel guilty for not being more effective in controlling him. So, they relieve their guilt and fear by "nagging" the child. They *tell* the child how to act. Then, if anything disastrous happens, they can say "We did our duty. We tried to tell him, but he just wouldn't listen."

"Nagging" (verbal warnings and advice) is a poor strategy for controlling a child's behavior. Not only does it fail to have positive effects; it has several negative effects, as anyone who has been "nagged" can testify. Suppose your husband often (but not always) tells you to limit your phone calls. Or, your wife keeps after you to cut the grass. If you submit to the nagging, you feel resentful and angry. Quite commonly you find it impossible to submit. The phone calls and the grass get longer and longer. Your mate has set a rule and, without quite realizing it, you are testing the rule, just like Johnny or Mary when you established a "chore rule." When parents nag their children, they are usually genuinely concerned about their development. They don't want their children to hate them; and they would rather the children didn't have to test the rules they lay down. But "nagging" isn't the answer to their problem. An alternative is described in the following section.

A mother is *not* responsible for everything her child does. She is *not* responsible for the consequences of her child's behavior. It is true that a parent has done much to make her child into the kind of person he is. But it is the *child*, not the parent, who must take responsibility for his actions. The parent is not responsible for controlling all of her child's behavior for the simple reason that it is impossible for her to do so.

The parent, however, *is* responsible for doing what she can do effectively. She is responsible for creating an environment in which the child can grow. She can do this by enforcing limits consistently. She can do this by providing a model for the child to follow. She can do this by allowing the child to discover things for himself. She can do this by freeing the child from the guilt which comes from being expected to follow rules that are impractical or impossible to follow.

LEARNING FOR YOURSELF

A child must learn for himself the consequences of his actions. That is not only the *best* way for him to learn—it is the *only* way he can learn. (That is why he *has* to break a rule you establish. In that instance, you provide the consequence.) In the cases below, which person is likely to learn something important?

106
a. Marie puts off her homework until 10:00. She doesn't have time to finish it.
b. Charles' father tells him "If you don't get busy on that homework, you won't finish it."

107
a. David has to find something on ants for a school report. Mother finds the appropriate section in the encyclopedia and reads it with him.
b. Donna has to make a report. Her mother points out the index volume of the encyclopedia.

108
a. Howard fell out of the apple tree.
b. Henry's mother called to him "Get out of that tree. You'll break your neck."

109
a. Minnie was late for school.
b. Penny's mother warned her to hurry.

110
a. Mrs. Black told Mr. Black that, when he writes a check, he must enter the amount on the stub.
b. Mr. Black's check "bounced" because he failed to enter another check he wrote.

NATURAL CONSEQUENCES OF BEHAVIORS

Many of the rules which parents try to enforce have natural consequences, other than the parent's response. Since these consequences operate even when the parent is not present, they provide a much more effective enforcement than the parent can provide. Whenever possible, then, it is efficient for the parent to let the child learn from the natural consequences of a behavior. The parent need not even state the rule. The child will formulate it for himself.

In each item below, choose the rule which would be effectively enforced by natural consequences. That is, a parent need not be present to enforce the rule. (To decide, ask yourself "What happens if the child breaks the rule?")

111
a. Do the dishes every Saturday night.
b. Do the dishes before the food hardens on them.

112
a. Don't hit the baby.
b. Don't hit the neighbor boy (same age and size).

113
a. Eat your dinner.
b. Wash your hands before dinner.

114
a. Don't stay up late because you have to get up at 6:00.
b. Empty the garbage before you come to bed.

115
a. Take your vitamins.
b. Don't put that sand in your mouth.

UNNECESSARY AND IMPRACTICAL RULES

Many of the rules which parents try to enforce are unnecessary and impractical. Consider whether you actually follow the rule now (not whether your mother told you to follow it when you were 10). Consider whether there is likely to be any benefit from the rule aside from "self-discipline." ("Self-discipline" can be imposed only by oneself.) Consider whether the result of breaking the rule is likely to be as disastrous as alleged. Consider whether it is worth the effort to enforce it consistently.

In the light of these considerations, look at the rules below. In each pair, pick one that is probably unnecessary or impractical.

116
a. Eat everything on your plate, or no dessert.
b. Wash your hands before you eat.

117
a. Look both ways before you cross the street.
b. Spend one hour every night reading for self-improvement.

118
a. Don't hide in empty refrigerators.
b. Don't get angry with your brother.

119
a. Don't masturbate.
b. Don't eat strange fruits and berries.

120
a. Don't get into a car with a stranger.
b. Don't wet your bed.

121
a. Go out and play, but don't get dirty.
b. Don't take things that don't belong to you.

122
a. Any time you get in trouble at school, tell me.
b. Finish your homework before you watch TV.

123
a. Don't play in the street.
b. Sit up straight.

EATING AND SLEEPING PROBLEMS

Many of the problems of young people are connected with eating and sleeping. In attacking these problems you would do well to look first at the environment. Making it safer and more comfortable is often enough to solve the problem. If you still find it necessary to establish a rule, the rule will be easier to enforce if the environment is safe.

EATING PROBLEMS

A stable environment is safe and comfortable. Consistency in the environment makes it safer and more comfortable. Therefore, dinner time can be made more comfortable by introducing some regularity. If there are some predictable things about the dinner table, the child will like to come there. Which of the suggestions below will make dinner time more comfortable? (Choose *a* or *b*.)

124
a. Never use a tablecloth.
b. Sometimes use a tablecloth, sometimes don't.

125
a. Eat whenever Dad gets hungry.
b. Establish a regular time for dinner.

126
a. Provide variety by sitting in a different place every night.
b. Provide uniformity by a special place for each member of the family.

127
a. Mention beforehand what you are fixing for dinner.
b. Keep the menu a secret and surprise the family.

128
a. Enforce one reasonable rule at the dinner table.
b. Watch the children closely to detect any bad manners.

One effect of tension in some people is loss of appetite. After you have done something to make dinner time more predictable, there will be less tension at mealtime. There are other ways to lessen the tension. The dinner table is a good place for conversation. But often it becomes a sounding board for any member of the family who has a complaint. Which of the topics of conversation below is likely to create a *more comfortable* atmosphere at mealtime?

129
a. Johnny's latest misbehavior.
b. Suzy's latest accomplishment.

130
a. Suzy's poor eating habits.
b. The tastiness of the main dish.

131
a. Dad's troubles at work.
b. The progress of the new freeway.

132
a. The funny thing that happened at school.
b. Johnny's complaints about the neighbor boy.

133
a. The problems arising from U.S. foreign policy.
b. The financial problems of the family.

134
If someone brings up an unpleasant topic of conversation, which is the best method of handling the situation?
a. Say "Let's not talk about that. It's not the right kind of talk for the dinner table."
b. Ignore it. Continue talking about the prior topic, or bring up a new one.

The kinds of rules which parents try to enforce at the dinner table are often unreasonable and unenforceable. Parents are concerned about their child's nutrition, of course, but forcing a child to eat a particular food, or punishing him when he doesn't, is not the way to build healthy eating habits. It is a *good* way to build an aversion to foods. Instead, provide your child with a variety of good foods. Let him decide what he will eat, and how much. (If he eats very little, and you worry a lot, give him a vitamin pill every morning. Not eating probably won't hurt him.) Which rules below are consistent with the principle *Provide a variety of foods and let your child decide what to eat and how much?*

135
a. "You must finish your peas before you can have more peas."
b. "You must finish your peas before you can have more meat."

136
a. "You may not have dessert until you eat all your dinner."
b. "You may not come back to the table after you have left."

137
a. Suzy must eat at least one bite of everything.
b. Mother must put a little bit of everything on Suzy's plate.

Sometimes parents encourage eating problems by "catering" to them. In an extreme instance, Mother fixes a different meal for every member of the family. It is easy to see how such problems arise. When Suzy is six months old, Mother offers her spinach. It tastes strange, and Suzy refuses it. Mother tries again a few days later. Suzy refuses again. Mother concludes that Suzy doesn't like spinach. She talks about Suzy's aversion to spinach. She never fixes spinach for Suzy. As soon as Suzy is old enough to understand, she learns that she doesn't like spinach. She sometimes wonders how spinach tastes.

A child refuses a new food because it looks strange or tastes unusual. Sometimes he just doesn't feel like eating a particular food. (Many adults who like eggs cannot tolerate them on some days.) It is not reasonable to conclude that a child has a permanent dislike for a food because he rejects it on a few occasions. Continue to offer the food. The child may eventually decide he likes it.

Which of the choices below is consistent with this position?

138 | If you are serving something you are sure Johnny won't eat:
a. Fix something else for him.
b. Include at least one food in the menu that he *will* like.

139 | If Johnny did not eat anything at all:
a. Allow him to fix himself a bowl of cereal before he goes to bed.
b. Allow him to rummage in the refrigerator while you are eating dinner.

SLEEPING PROBLEMS

When children are tense and frightened, they can't eat. Neither can they sleep. When there are problems at bedtime, look first at the environment. If the environment is safe and comfortable, such problems will be less likely to occur.

A child relaxes when he knows what's coming next. Introducing consistency into the bedtime routine is the first step in attacking these problems. Which of the choices below will make bedtime more predictable?

140	a. Day 1: Bath, pajamas, teeth, water, toilet Day 2: Bath, teeth, toilet, pajamas, water Day 3: Teeth, pajamas, story Day 4: Pajamas, teeth, lullaby b. Day 1: Pajamas, toilet, story, water Day 2: Pajamas, toilet, story, water Day 3: Pajamas, toilet, story, water Day 4: Pajamas, toilet, story, water

141	a. Have your spouse oversee the routine sometimes. b. Always oversee the routine yourself, if at all possible.

142	a. Establish a consistent time as bedtime. b. Put the child to bed when he seems to be tired.

143	a. Read a familiar story at bedtime. b. Read a new story every night.

144	a. Provide a variety of night clothes. b. Provide similar-appearing night clothes.

Many children refuse to go to bed, or refuse to stay there. Others cry or make numerous demands on their parents when they are put to bed. These children are tense and frightened, although they often appear to be brash, lively, willful, or winning. They will relax during the performance of a predictable routine. When a child is very fearful, a warm bath is particularly comforting. Listening to a story which he knows well is also relaxing. Establishing a bedtime routine is very much like establishing a rule. A child must test it before he can depend on it. Be prepared, then, to enforce the routine as you would a rule.

Include in the routine all the necessities, like going to the bathroom and drinking some water. Then you will feel better about ignoring the "irrelevant" demands after the child is in bed.

Aside from establishing a routine to help the child relax, you can make other changes in the environment to make it safer. Which of the changes below would make a fearful child more comfortable?

145 a. Put the child in a room with an older brother or sister (they get along well).
b. Put the child in a room by himself.

146 a. Make the room as dark as possible.
b. Leave the door open a crack, or use a night light.

147 a. Put guard rails on the bed.
b. Insist that the child use a "grown-up" bed.

148 a. Close the closet before you leave.
b. Go in often, without warning, to check on things.

After you have established a routine, and have made the bedroom as safe as possible, it is necessary to remove possible sources of stimulation. Which of the following choices would reduce stimulation and encourage sleep in a wakeful child?

149
a. Give him warm milk before bed.
b. Give him a cola before bed (cola, like coffee, contains caffeine).

150
a. Invite company to come as soon as the child is in bed.
b. Invite company to come after the child has had some time to go to sleep.

151
a. Turn down radio, television, or record player until the child is asleep.
b. Keep the volume on those items high so the child will learn to sleep in a noisy place.

152
a. Draw the curtains and shades.
b. Leave the curtains and shades open.

When children share the same room, they commonly stimulate each other. They tell stories, gossip, invent games. Which of the measures below might reduce this problem?

| 153 | a. Put them to bed at the same time.
b. Establish a different bedtime for each child. |

| 154 | a. Put them to bed at the same time, but put one in your bed until a later time.
b. Put them to bed at the same time, but tell them not to talk. |

| 155 | a. Leave the door open so you can hear if they fool around.
b. Put a screen or some furniture between their beds. |

After you have done everything in your power to make the environment safe, predictable, and nonstimulating, it is time to handle the problem behaviors. Which method of handling the behaviors described below is consistent with the methods described in this program?

156	Matthew gets out of bed and plays.
	a. When you hear him get out of bed, tell him to get back in bed. If he doesn't get back quickly, spank him.
	b. Listen carefully and, whenever he gets out of bed, put him back in bed. Say "It's not time to get up yet."

157	Mary cries and screams when she is put in bed.
	a. Since the environment is now as safe as possible, consider her crying to be an irrelevant behavior. Ignore it. Do not respond and it will cease after some testing.
	b. Since Mary is crying, she must not be ready to sleep. Let her get up and play until she is tired.

158	Mark keeps asking for things after he is put in bed. He wants water, cookie, the light on, the light off, more covers, etc.
	a. His asking for things indicates an unfulfilled need. Give him what he asks for, if you think it is reasonable, and eventually he will feel satisfied and will go to sleep.
	b. Since you have made the environment as comfortable as possible, assume that his demands are irrelevant. Do not answer him and eventually he will relax and go to sleep.

159	Luke and Logan spend 5 to 10 minutes talking before they go to sleep.
	a. Insist that they not talk, since a problem might arise if you don't keep control of things.
	b. Since they regularly go to sleep after 5 or 10 minutes, ignore the talking. If their talking becomes a problem, that is time enough to institute a rule.

MORAL TRAINING:
LEARNING RIGHT FROM WRONG

All parents worry from time to time about teaching their children right from wrong. Many are unsure themselves of what constitutes right and wrong. May a starving man steal? Does insanity excuse a man from responsibility for moral behavior? And what about abortion, euthanasia, capital punishment, and war? The confusion and argument arising from these questions is disheartening. A parent can't wait until the philosophers have settled the issues. He has to train his child today to act appropriately tomorrow.

Suppose it were possible to make a list of all the situations in which a child will be required to select the right action. We could then tell him what to do in every case. Perhaps then there would be no problem of moral training. But clearly this solution is impossible. We must, instead, enable a child to make wise decisions, to select the better alternative when he has a choice. The task, then, is to train morality by training decision making. For, whatever else morality may be, it at least includes making wise decisions.

Children (and adults, too) will make wise decisions to the extent that they are aware of the consequences of those decisions. Every act has a consequence. Dropping a glass is followed by a crash. Eating an apple is followed by a reduction of hunger. Touching the hot stove is followed by pain. These are examples of "personal" consequences. Many acts also have social consequences. Dropping the glass may be followed by a scolding from Mother. Touching the stove may be followed by a verbal warning about hot objects. It is from these social consequences of actions that a child learns what is right and what is wrong.

Consider the following situation.

---

160 | Billy is taking a test. He can't remember the answer to question 5. He looks at John's paper, sees the answer, and copies it. What is the personal consequence of his behavior?
  a. He stops worrying about question 5.
  b. His memory is improved.

---

161 | What is the likely social consequence of his behavior?
  a. His teacher will congratulate him on his resourcefulness.
  b. His teacher will lecture to him on honesty and integrity, and possibly punish him.

Here is another situation.

---

162 | Mary shows Suzanne her new bracelet, then lays it on the table. Later Suzanne takes the bracelet, hides it in her purse, and takes it home with her. What is the personal consequence of this behavior?
  a. Mary does not invite Suzanne to her home again.
  b. Suzanne's desire for the bracelet is gratified.

To make a decision, a child should be able to predict the most likely consequence of his action. If his information is accurate and sufficient, he will make a wise decision. This assumption may seem unreasonably optimistic in the light of the numerous unwise decisions people make every day. But let us assume, if only for the sake of argument, that people *can* act wisely and will do so if their information is sufficient. When someone makes an unwise decision, then, it is because he lacks relevant information.

Some of the consequences of behavior are apparent immediately. (Eating a stolen cookie satisfies an immediate hunger. Mother's harsh look, the scolding, and the punishment occur as soon as she misses the cookie.) Other consequences are delayed. (Mother puts the cookie jar on a higher shelf when she refills it.) A delayed consequence typically has little influence on the behavior of a very young child. It becomes increasingly important as he matures.

Consider the following situation.

163	Bobby's gang decides to skip school. There is an important test in English class, but Bobby goes along with the others. What *immediate* consequence might he realistically predict?
	a. Bobby will be exhilarated and secure in the approval of his group.
	b. Bobby's teacher will dismiss the rest of the class since he is not there.

164	What *delayed* consequence might he predict?
	a. He will be selected "Honor Citizen of the Year."
	b. His grade will be lowered since he will miss a crucial test.

Here is another situation.

---

165 | Diane promised to have the car home by eleven o'clock. She can't make it unless she speeds and takes some dangerous chances while driving. She decides to try it. As a consequence, she is given a ticket for speeding. Is this consequence of speeding
a. Immediate?
b. Delayed?

---

166 | Since paying for the ticket wiped out her savings, she is unable to buy the new dress she wanted for the school dance. Is this consequence of speeding
a. Immediate?
b. Delayed?

The consequences of behavior are personal or social, immediate or delayed. To make a wise decision, one must be able to predict what is likely to happen and how seriously the consequences will affect him.

Inadequate prediction of immediate consequences is responsible for many unwise decisions. Some people are unduly influenced by the personal consequences of behavior. They are impulsive, impetuous, and apparently unconcerned with the reactions of those around them. The social psychopath, acting purely on the basis of momentary gratification, is an extreme example. The anxiety-driven neurotic is more common. He is not so much *unconcerned* as *unaware* of others' responses. His immediate needs are too great to permit him to notice other people's reactions to him.

For others, acute sensitivity to the responses of other people is accompanied by an unhealthy disregard for personal consequences. In a frantic attempt to please (or punish) other people, they consistently make decisions harmful to themselves. Take, for example, the eager housewife who can't say no to any request for her help. Or the rebellious college student who systematically breaks every rule of the code her parents cherish, and makes certain that they are aware of it.

Delayed consequences are especially hard to predict. How can a young girl estimate the amount of guilt she will suffer after her abortion? How can the heavy drinker predict the pain of diseases to which his body becomes vulnerable? In both cases there may be no distress; on the other hand, the distress may be considerable. Delayed consequences may also be pleasant, but again it is difficult to judge. To what extent will the broken marriage result in contentment and increased peace of mind? Will winning the "war of liberation" result in peace and prosperity for the people? In each case positive consequences may outweigh negative consequences. Or they may not. Naive and inaccurate predictions of delayed consequences are responsible for numerous unwise (immoral) decisions by individuals as well as by business and government.

How can a parent train a child to make wise decisions? The child must be prepared to respond to the social consequences of his actions—but he must weigh these against the personal consequences before making a decision. He must balance the immediate consequences against a realistic assessment of the delayed consequences.

The parent's responsibility is to arrange conditions so that the necessary information is available and usable. The parent provides:

1. A model of moral behavior.
2. Accurate information about the child's behavior.
3. Information about the delayed consequences of behavior.
4. Freedom to develop an effective conscience.

THE PARENT AS A MODEL

When a child has a choice in a situation, he acts the way he thinks some model would act. The model might be a brother or sister, a neighbor child, a schoolmate, a TV hero. But by far the most influential models in a child's life are his parents.

Therefore a child's principal source of information about conduct is his parent's behavior. By listening to his parents, he learns how they want him to act. By watching his parents, he learns how they act. The two are often not the same. He is more likely to behave as his parents behave rather than as they tell him to behave since we learn primarily by example. Thus, first and foremost, a parent must provide a model of the behavior he wishes to encourage.

Some parental behaviors are described below. In each case determine the more probable effect on the child.

---

167 | Mr. Jones insists that Jimmy cross the street at the corner and look both ways. He has warned him about darting between parked cars. Mr. Jones is an excellent, careful driver. He observes traffic laws. Occasionally, however, when he is in a big hurry and, if there is no traffic, he will "drift" through a stop light or sign. As an adult, Jimmy will
  a. Observe all traffic laws scrupulously.
  b. Observe traffic laws when it is convenient.

---

168 | Mrs. Smith takes very good care of her children. She feeds them hot meals and vitamins and dresses them warmly in cold weather. She often neglects to eat breakfast or lunch because she is rushed and, instead, has a snack when there is time. As an adult, Janie Smith will
  a. Feed her children well, but neglect her own nutritional needs.
  b. Eat well-balanced, hot meals and vitamins.

In the cases below, predict what the child will probably do:

---

169 | Mother cuddles and sings to the new baby. Janet has a new doll. She will
    a. Scold the doll.
    b. Cuddle and sing to the doll.

---

170 | When Dad wants Jimmy to do something, he yells at him. Jimmy wants his sister to open the door for him. He will
    a. Yell at his sister.
    b. Ask her politely to open the door.

---

171 | Mom is always telling Greg to say "Thank you" and "Please." Greg brings Mom the newspaper. She says, "Oh, I didn't know it was here." Mom wants help with the groceries. She says "Help me with these bags." Mom wants to see Greg's school paper. She says "Let me see it, Greg." The next-door neighbor gives Greg a cookie. He will
    a. Say "Thank you."
    b. Not say "Thank you."

---

172 | Greg wants another cookie. He will
    a. Say "Please."
    b. Not say "Please."

173 | When Mom and Dad argue, Mom usually winds up crying. Mary and Jack are arguing. Mary will
  a. Cry.
  b. Hit Jack on the head.

174 | Mother tells George that he must eat his dinner if he wants to grow big and strong. When George is an adult he will
  a. Tell his son to eat his dinner in order to grow big and strong.
  b. Allow his child to eat what he wants.

Which would be the most effective way to solve the problems below?

175 | Steven is always hitting other children.
  a. Tell Steven it is not nice to hit others.
  b. Stop spanking Steven.

176 | Marlene has been swearing a lot.
  a. Stop swearing yourself.
  b. Require Marlene to write an essay on the evils of cursing.

177 | Ronald has taken up smoking.
  a. Stop smoking yourself.
  b. Explain the dangers of smoking.

Moral decisions usually concern adherence to the rules of the culture in which one lives. A mother teaches her child, by her example, to live within the rules or, alternatively, to ignore the rules. Since a child does not *know* the rules of the adult world, he can hardly judge the extent to which his parents observe these rules. It is not surprising that the parent of a delinquent child often complains "But I never even got a traffic ticket. I don't steal, or kill, or commit adultery." The child learns about rules in a different world—primarily the world of home. A parent makes a rule for a child, then neglects to enforce it. The child learns that rules are undependable, sometime things. If Mother respected the rule, she would enforce it. If she does not respect a rule she made herself, what rule *is* worthy of respect? It is difficult, but important, to remember that the casual rule about making your bed after breakfast is equivalent in a child's world to an adult law about declaring all of your income on a tax return.

THE PARENT AS A MIRROR OF BEHAVIOR

Children (and some adults) are relatively unaware of their own behaviors. They do not see themselves as others see them. A child's garbled and inaccurate reconstruction of an event is probably a correct reflection of what she *thinks* happened. A parent, then, performs a valuable function when he tells the child what actually did happen. But the parent's account must be as objective as possible. Otherwise the child merely substitutes the parent's emotional distortion for her own. She still doesn't know what happened.

Unfortunately, parents are usually not very objective in reflecting reality to a child. They teach the child a series of rationalizations which "fog up" the decision making process. These rationalizations teach the child to look at *who* did an act and *why* he did it rather than *what* he did and *what* its consequences will be. For example:

When a child hits another child, it is not acceptable.
But when an adult hits a child, it is called "spanking."
Spanking is acceptable.

Or:

When a good guy kills a bad guy, it is called "justice."
When a bad guy kills a good guy, it is called "crime."

Thus, a child comes to believe that, regardless of consequences, an action is all right if its motive is acceptable. That is, an act is incorrectly assumed to be moral if it can be described in socially acceptable terms.

A parent can help his children avoid this error by describing an act with neutral words rather than emotionally charged words. The "emotional" words tend to describe some assumed motive for an act rather than the act itself. They indicate acceptance or rejection to the child, but do not increase his information about the act. In the following pairs of sentences, which one is more nearly *neutral* or objective as a description of an act.

178

a. It was a boyish prank.	b. He broke the windows.
a. He refused to do the work.	b. He defied me.
a. I punished him for his own good.	b. I took away his car privileges.
a. She sassed me.	b. She said she didn't care for my opinion.
a. She's very high strung.	b. She gets angry very easily.
a. He killed the girl.	b. He butchered the girl.
a. It was a mild flirtation.	b. I dated her several times.
a. She copied my work.	b. She cheated.
a. He squandered his fortune.	b. He spent all his money.

179

Your 6-year-old brings home her playmate's toy. In the alternative responses below, one is accepting, one rejecting, and one neutral (objective). Which should you say to reflect her behavior objectively?

a. "You have 'borrowed' John's toy. Now it is time to return it."

b. "You have 'taken' John's toy. You may not take things that belong to other people. You must return it."

c. "You have 'stolen' John's toy. Stealing is very bad. Return the toy immediately."

Here is another situation.

180 | Your son has just "clobbered" his playmate. Soon they are both crying and appealing to you. What should you say?
- a. "Billy, you hit Kenny, but it was an accident. It won't happen again, will it, Billy?"
- b. "Billy, you are a bad boy to hit Kenny. Tell him you are sorry."
- c. "Billy, you hit Kenny. Did it hurt you, Kenny?"

THE PARENT AS SEER

As a child grows, she learns to predict the immediate consequences of her behavior. The more delayed the consequence, however, the less likely she is to attribute it to her action. Parents can contribute valuable information about the more remote consequences of actions. Unfortunately, parents are usually no more accurate in their description of the consequences of an act than they are in their description of the act itself. Mother tells Carole that, if she doesn't share her dolls, her playmates won't like her anymore. Carole does not share her dolls, but she still has friends. Dad tells George that women appreciate a man who treats them with courtesy. George is always polite, but is aware that the girls consider him "square." Misinformation about consequences is probably worse than no information. If she is misinformed, a child will understandably begin to ignore any information she receives about consequences.

Parents do not purposely misinform their children. The confusion often arises from an attempt to apply the rules of adult conduct to children's conduct. "Hitting," for example, is not acceptable for adults. There are laws against it. A man who attacks with his fists instead of his tongue is rejected or, at least, considered immature by his associates. But hitting has different consequences for children. Skill in fighting may bring admiration from one's peers. On the other hand, hitting can have negative consequences. The victim may hit back. Most children discover this for themselves. What a child may not discover—until it is too late—is that he is capable of hurting another person. It *is* appropriate to reflect this possibility to him.

The rules of one generation may be inappropriate for the next generation. The rules of conduct in Georgia may not apply in Michigan or California. *Parents must look at what actually happens rather than what is supposed to happen if the information is to be useful to their child.*

---

181 | Which of the following is a more accurate statement of consequences?
- a. If you have sexual relations before marriage, no "decent" boy will marry you.
- b. If you have sexual relations before marriage, you may get pregnant.

---

182 | Which of these is more probable?
- a. If you use drugs, you may come to rely on them to escape problems.
- b. If you use drugs, you will become a drug addict and destroy your life.

---

183 | Which of these?
- a. If you don't clean up your room now, Santa Claus won't bring you any toys.
- b. If you don't clean up your room now, you will miss dinner.

THE PARENT AND THE CONSCIENCE

Probably anyone could play tennis if he received expert training and practiced assiduously. But if he seldom sets foot on a tennis court, he remains a beginner. So it is with conscience—that complex series of evaluation devices that guide our decision making processes. An effective conscience cannot develop unless a child is allowed to use it. In other words, a child must be free to *explore situations, make decisions, and suffer the consequences.* That is how a conscience grows.

In the situations below, which alternative allows the child freedom to explore social situations?

---

184 | Your teenager has been invited to a party. He is flattered and anxious to attend. But you have heard unsavory stories about the parties given by this group. Which course of action allows freedom to explore?
   a. Allow him to attend the party.
   b. Forbid his attendance.

---

185 | Your son wants to try out for Little League baseball. He is the most uncoordinated child you know. You are certain that he will be embarrassed at practice and will sit on the bench during games. If he is to be free to explore, what should you do?
   a. Allow him to try out.
   b. Interest him in stamp collecting instead.

---

186 | Your daughter has a new girl friend. The girl has a bad reputation. What should you do?
   a. Forbid your daughter to associate with her.
   b. Remain neutral about the association.

A child cannot become trustworthy unless he has an opportunity to do wrong. The impulse to protect your children is strong. But "protection" which leaves a child spineless is of questionable value. It may be comforting to remind yourself that very, very few mistakes have really disasterous consequences. And even serious mistakes, made by otherwise healthy people, have a way of leaving the victim stronger and less likely to make mistakes in the future.

In which situation below is the child being allowed to *make his own decisions?*

	a	**b**
187	Bill: I saw a boy cheating on a test today at school. Should I report it? Dad: What happens if you do? Bill: He will be mad at me, for one thing. The other kids don't like cheating, but I don't think they would appreciate my telling on him. You know—"tattling" and all that. The teacher might be happy to know what is going on. But he might be embarrassed about it, too. Dad: What happens if you don't report? Bill: His high grade might affect the "curve," but not much, I guess. He will be more likely to cheat on the next test and maybe less likely to study for it. If his conscience is bothering him, it will continue to. Dad: What do you think you ought to do?	Bill: I saw a boy cheating on a test today at school. Should I report it? Dad: What he does really isn't your business, is it? He is the one who suffers in the long run. If you get involved, you will just make everyone mad at you. I'd stay out of it if I were you.

In which situation is the child free to *make her own decision?*

	a	b
188	**Julie:** Should I invite Martha to my party? I'm about the only friend she has. The other girls don't like her. **Mother:** If you don't invite her, she will be heartbroken. You don't want that on your conscience. You had better invite her. The other girls can stand it for one evening.	**Julie:** Should I invite Martha to my party? I'm about the only friend she has. The other girls don't like her. **Mother:** What happens if you don't? **Julie:** She will be awfully hurt. She might think I don't like her. But the other girls will feel more comfortable without her. I would probably be more relaxed, not worrying about how people are getting along. But I'll feel guilty for hurting her. **Mother:** What happens if you do invite her? **Julie:** The party will be strained and probably not much fun. Martha just doesn't know how to fit in a group. She'll be uncomfortable all evening. I'll feel guilty about making a situation where everyone is uncomfortable. **Mother:** It's your party. What will you do?

In which situation is the child being allowed to *suffer the consequences of her behavior?*

| 189 | Mrs. Brown discovers that Linda has walked out of the store with a candy bar she didn't pay for.
a. Mrs. Brown returns and pays for the candy.
b. Mrs. Brown gives Linda the money and sends her back to pay for it. Linda must repay her mother from her piggy bank. |

In which situation is the child allowed to *suffer the consequences of his behavior?*

| 190 | George was caught joy riding in a stolen car.
a. His parents rush to the police station, bail him out, and put pressure on the officials to drop the charges since it is his first offense. They promise to supervise him more closely.
b. His parents arrange bail and employ a competent attorney. It is understood that George will have to repay his parents the amount of the attorney's fee when the case is concluded. |

By this time the reader may suspect that the devil in the child is his vulnerability to control by the immediate consequences of his acts—and his ignorance of the delayed personal and social consequences. And these latter must be learned largely at first hand. Our job, as parents, is to provide information on demand. One evidence of our respect for the dignity of a child is our faith that he can profit from experience, thus achieving a morality superior to ours.

APPENDIX A
KEEPING A RECORD

When you make a rule for your child and enforce it consistently, you can expect a change in his behavior. One reason the technique is so powerful is that it involves consistent feedback to the child on his performance—a necessary condition for learning. Feedback is a critical factor in bringing about behavior change.

Parents usually do not enforce rules consistently, so this procedure requires a change in their own behavior. Thus, the parent also needs feedback on his rule-enforcing behavior and its effectiveness. For this reason, we recommend that you keep a chart until the new behavior is automatic with you, at least several weeks.

The following procedure will help you to chart your behavior as well as that of your child. Refer to the Record Sheet, which is on page 117.

STEP 1

Establish a rule. Write your rule in the box at the top of the Record Sheet.

STEP 2

How often can your rule be tested—several times a day or several times a week? (A monthly rule is not a good one for introductory purposes, as progress is very slow.)

Circle the correct phrase for *your* rule:
—several times a day
—several times a week

Depending on what you circled, write days or weeks in the box *under* the chart on the Record Sheet.

This tells you the time units you will use to chart progress.

You will see change most dramatically and quickly if your rule can be tested several times every day. If your rules can be tested only once every day, or less often than that, a weekly chart is needed.

More time will be required for visible change.

STEP 3

Chart your progress.

Tally boxes are provided on the Record Sheet for you to keep track of rule testing. Every time a rule is tested, make a mark in the appropriate tally box. If you enforced the rule, circle your tally. Keep the Record Sheet handy so that you may record events as soon as possible.

A typical tally box might look like this:

The rule was tested 6 times. It was enforced 4 times. (To be effective, rule enforcement should be 100%. This may take several days for the parent to achieve.)

At the end of the day (or week) count the tallies and transfer the information to the chart. You may chart both instances of rule testing and instances of rule enforcement, if they are different. The tally box above would look like this on a chart:

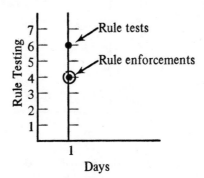

Several days' progress might look like this:

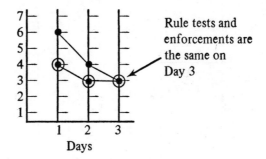

Rule tests and enforcements are the same on Day 3

Fill in the chart below, using the information from the tally box.

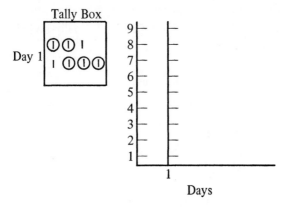

Fill in the 3-day chart below, using the tally boxes.

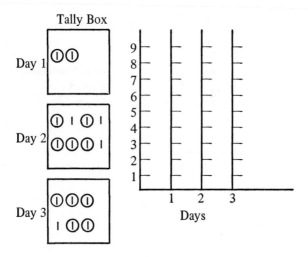

116

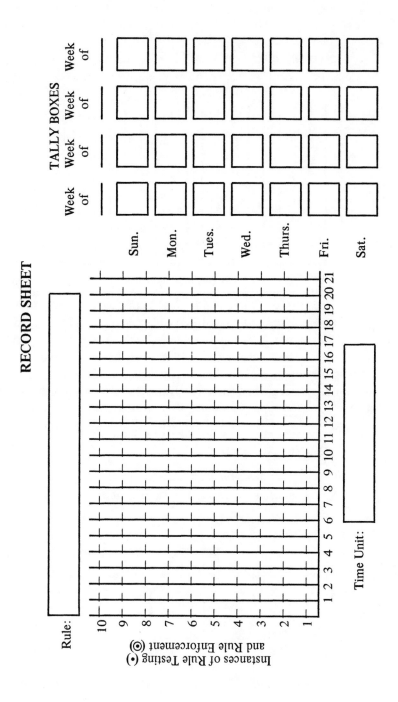

RECORD SHEET

Rule:

Instances of Rule Testing (•)
and Rule Enforcement (◎)

Time Unit:

TALLY BOXES

Week of | Week of | Week of | Week of

Sun.
Mon.
Tues.
Wed.
Thurs.
Fri.
Sat.

INTERPRETING A RECORD

A record of incidents of rule testing has this general shape.

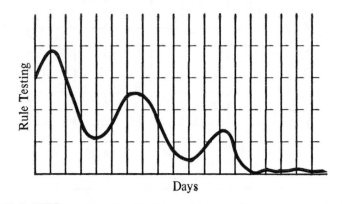

Notice that after an initial increase in rule testing, you can expect a sharp decrease. This is followed by another increase, usually less intense than the first "peak." The cycle continues with another decrease, a slight increase, etc. Finally rule testing reaches a very low level, and occurs only when something unusual makes the environment less predictable. Thus, rule testing is never completely extinguished, but remains at a very low level.

Your chart may look like the one above. If so, continue your actions. They are proving effective.

If your chart does *not* look like the one above, decide which one below is most similar and follow the action recommendations provided.

Variant A

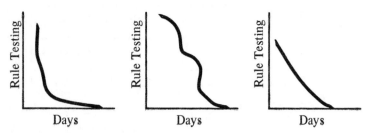

Interpretation

These charts indicate a relatively rapid decrease in rule testing. Such a chart usually indicates that the child is in a stable phase of her emotional development and is already accustomed to the rule enforcement procedures. (This chart might also occur if punishment were being administered, a condition which is *not* recommended as a part of this rule enforcement technique.)

Action
Continue.

Variant B

Interpretation

The curves above are actually the same as the general extinction curves described at the beginning of this section. The only difference is that there are not yet enough incidents for the shape to be apparent.

Action
Continue.

Variant C

Interpretation

These curves show that rule testing is not decreasing, but is increasing. If only a few days have been recorded, this could be the initial phase of the general extinction curve, i.e., an increase that will be followed by a sharp decrease.

If more than seven days have been recorded, these curves indicate that either (1) rule enforcement has been inconsistent, or (2) some consequence of the rule-testing behavior is extremely rewarding. (For example, the rule is that Mary must make her bed before school. When she tests the rule, she misses the school bus and Dad drives her to school. She enjoys having Dad drive her to school, and dislikes the school bus ride. Thus, her rule testing is rewarded and rule enforcement is not effective.)

Action

1. Check to determine whether you have been enforcing the rule consistently. Our research indicates that unless a rule is enforced *at least* 80% of the time, it has no effect on behavior. Of course, 100% enforcement is desirable. If you think that you will be unable to enforce the rule consistently, it is an unenforceable rule and will have to be abandoned for a better one.
2. If enforcement has been consistent, check to see what consequence could be maintaining the rule-testing behavior. If possible, remove the rewarding consequence. (For example, in the case above, Dad could stop driving Mary to school. She would have to take a taxi [using her own money], walk, or stay at home. Surprisingly, staying at home is very seldom rewarding to a child after she has done it once or twice.) If it is not possible to remove the rewarding consequence, the rule is unenforceable and will have to be abandoned for a better one.

Variant D

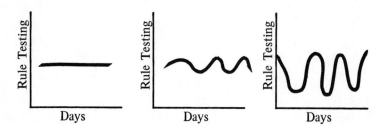

Interpretation

These curves show that rule testing is neither increasing nor decreasing. Rule enforcement has had no effect. The interpretation of these curves is the same as for Variant C, where rule testing increases.

Action

Same as for Variant C, above.

Appendix B

Classroom Application

Classroom teachers may wish to apply the techniques described in this program. A good way to begin is described below. (This method has also been found to be very effective in solving management problems in unruly classrooms.)

1. Set aside a 10-minute period at the same time every day for at least 2 weeks.
2. Select a task which all children can do without help. This might be free reading, workbook tasks, self-instructional or programmed tasks, reading, etc. Be sure that the slowest as well as the fastest children have work that they can do *successfully*.
3. Give the assignment(s) and say, "During the next 10 minutes you are to work by yourselves. I will not answer any questions. There will be one rule—No Talking."
4. During the next 10 minutes, do not respond to any irrelevant behavior. An "irrelevant behavior" is any behavior other than rule testing or task behavior. For example, hand raising, pencil dropping, gesturing, and daydreaming are all irrelevant behaviors. Do not respond to such behaviors by looking at the child, by speaking to him or by gesturing to him.

   Respond only to rule-testing behaviors; do it in the following way: Every time a child talks—for whatever reason—enforce the rule by saying "The rule please!" "What's the rule?" "No talking please," or something equivalent. Say the same thing every time.

A teacher is using the 10-minute procedure with his classroom. In each situation below, how should he respond?

---

1 | Brian noisily slams down his book and puts his head on his desk.
   a. Ignore his behavior.
   b. Say "Is something wrong, Brian?"

---

2 | Pam says "Mr. Brown, I didn't hear the assignment."
   a. Ignore her behavior.
   b. Say "The rule, please."

---

3 | Joe comes to your desk and asks if he is doing his assignment correctly.
   a. Ignore his behavior.
   b. Say "The rule, please."

---

4 | Linda comes to your desk and stands there quietly waiting to be noticed.
   a. Ignore her behavior.
   b. Say "The rule, please."

Which behavior below should he ignore?

---

5 | a. Mark raises his hand.
   b. Jean says "I don't understand this!"

---

6 | a. Billy asks his neighbor on what page the lesson begins.
   b. George marches ostentatiously to the waste basket 12 times in 10 minutes.

---

7 | a. Mary Ann starts reading her lesson aloud.
   b. Marsha bursts into tears.

5. During the 2-week period you will notice a sharp rise in rule-testing behaviors and irrelevant behaviors. If you respond consistently, these behaviors will extinguish and task behavior will increase. It is helpful and enlightening for the teacher to keep a record of behavior during the experimental period to aid in evaluation of the technique. In some cases it is possible to record behavior of an entire class. More commonly, teachers select one or two children who tend to be most distractible and record their behaviors in detail. Here are some alternatives:

a. Record each instance of rule testing during the 10-minute work session. Tabulate these behaviors and make a graph of their incidence each day, during the 2-week period.

b. Observe the most common kinds of irrelevant behavior. Record the incidence of these behaviors during the 10-minute work session. Tabulate and make a graph of these behaviors for the 2-week period.

c. Record with cumulative stop watch the amount of time a particular child spends actually working on this task. Make a graph from this data.

SUMMARY

1. Set aside a 10-minute work session.
2. Give an assignment that each child can do independently.
3. State the rule.
4. Enforce the rule consistently and ignore irrelevant behaviors.
5. Keep a record of behavior during each session.

APPENDIX C
THE PURPOSE OF A RULE

Detailed in *Child Management* are a number of techniques for bringing about changes in behavior. The techniques involve consistent enforcement of a rule or routine.

The purpose of the rule may appear to be control or manipulation of some behavior. Behavior is, indeed, modified. But as a purpose, such control would be trivial. The purpose of the rule is to create a better, safer, more comfortable environment. There are *many* ways to manipulate behavior. Some are probably as efficient as the ones we describe. It is the element of *consistency* which is the key to a safer (i.e., more predictable) environment.

We have taken the position that, with just a few, very stable "cornerstones of consistency," a child (or adult) will be free to explore the vast, unpredictable areas of his environment. Watch as Mother takes her one-year-old to visit a neighbor. The baby first huddles in Mother's lap. After a while she takes three steps out and returns to hide between Mother's knees. Later she takes five steps and comes back to touch her knee. Gradually, her circle of exploration expands and every so often she returns just to touch Mother. Mother is the consistency. She is tested, and remains the same. Her predictability reduces the child's anxiety to a manageable level. The child can use her "ego strength" to learn new things.

The consistency of a rule or routine is like the consistency of Mother's appearance and behavior in the example above. It is an easily, safely tested handle on the world. It is as though the child said, "If a few things remain dependable, I can deal with the undependable."

There are several consequences of this view of the purpose of rules.

1. If you see a rule as a way of controlling behavior, you will need to have many rules to control the many behaviors children exhibit. If you see a rule as creating a safe environment, you need have very few rules.

2. If a rule is primarily to manipulate behavior, the content of the rule is crucial. If the rule is to create an environment, the content is relatively unimportant. As long as the rule meets the criteria detailed in *Child Management*, it doesn't matter if it is "Empty the trash before 6:00," or "Ring the bell three times before entering the house."

3. If a rule is to control behavior, some effective methods of shaping might be employed in its enforcement. Verbal or material payoffs might be employed. Punishments might be invoked.

   If a rule is to create an environment, nothing is gained by the use of such devices. The rule can be effectively enforced without them. And the child may be less dependent, more self-reliant, as a result.

ANSWER KEY

1 a (b)

2 (a) b

3 (a) b

4 a (b)

5 (a) b

6 (a) b

7 (a) b

8 (a) b

9 a (b)

10 (a) b

11 a (b)

12 a (b)

13 a (b)

14 (a) b

15 (a) b

16 a (b)

17 (a) b

18 (a) b

19 a (b)

20 (a) b

21 a (b)

22 a (b)

23 (a) b

24 a (b)

25 (a) b

26 (a) b

27 (a) b

28 a (b)

29 a (b)

30 (a) b

31 (a) b

32 a (b)

33 (a) b

34 a (b)

35 a (b)

36 (a) b

37 (a) b

38 a (b)

39 (a) b

40 (a) b

41 a (b)

42 (a) b

43 a (b)

44 (a) b

45 (a) b

46 a (b)

47 (a) b

48 a (b)

49 a (b)

50 a (b)

51...........
....
....

52 (a) b

53 a (b)

54 (a) b

55 (a) b

56 (a) b

57 a (b)

58 (a) b

59 a (b)

60 a (b)

61 a (b)

62 Enforce
the rule....
....

63 (a) b

64 a (b)

65 (a) b

66 (a) b

67 a (b)

68 a (b)

69 (a) b

70 (a) b

71 a **(b)**   89 a **(b)**   108 **(a)** b   127 **(a)** b

72 **(a)** b   90 a **(b)**   109 **(a)** b   128 **(a)** b

73 **(a)** b   91 **(a)** b   110 a **(b)**   129 a **(b)**

74 a **(b)**   92 **(a)** b   111 a **(b)**   130 a **(b)**

75 a **(b)**   93 **(a)** b   112 a **(b)**   131 a **(b)**

76 a **(b)**   94 a **(b)**   113 **(a)** b   132 **(a)** b

77 **(a)** b   95 **(a)** b   114 **(a)** b   133 **(a)** b

78 **(a)** b   96 a **(b)**   115 a **(b)**   134 a **(b)**

79 a **(b)**   97 a **(b)**   116 **(a)** b   135 **(a)** b

80 **(a)** b   98 a **(b)**   117 a **(b)**   136 a **(b)**

81 a **(b)**   99 **(a)** b   118 a **(b)**   137 a **(b)**

82 a **(b)**   100 **(a)** b   119 **(a)** b   138 a **(b)**

83 **(a)** b   101 **(a)** b   120 a **(b)**   139 **(a)** b

84 a **(b)**   102 **(a)** b   121 **(a)** b   140 a **(b)**

85...........   103 **(a)** b   122 **(a)** b   141 a **(b)**
....
....   104 a **(b)**   123 a **(b)**   142 **(a)** b

86 **(a)** b   105 a **(b)**   124 **(a)** b   143 **(a)** b

87 a **(b)**   106 **(a)** b   125 a **(b)**   144 a **(b)**

88 **(a)** b   107 a **(b)**   126 a **(b)**   145 **(a)** b

146 a **b**	165 **a** b	**a** b	**Appendix B**
147 **a** b	166 a **b**	**a** b	1 **a** b
148 **a** b	167 a **b**	a **b**	2 a **b**
149 **a** b	168 **a** b	179 a **b** c	3 a **b**
150 a **b**	169 a **b**	180 a b **c**	4 **a** b
151 **a** b	170 **a** b	181 a **b**	5 **a** b
152 **a** b	171 a **b**	182 **a** b	6 a **b**
153 a **b**	172 a **b**	183 a **b**	7 a **b**
154 **a** b	173 **a** b	184 **a** b	
155 a **b**	174 **a** b	185 **a** b	
156 a **b**	175 a **b**	186 a **b**	
157 **a** b	176 **a** b	187 **a** b	
158 a **b**	177 **a** b	188 a **b**	
159 a **b**	178 a **b**	189 a **b**	
160 **a** b	**a** b	190 a **b**	
161 a **b**	a **b**		
162 a **b**	a **b**		
163 **a** b	a **b**		
164 a **b**	**a** b		

73